General editor: Graham Handley MA

Brodie's Notes on William Goldin

Rites of Passage

Peter Washington

Senior Tutor and Deputy Head, The Graduate Centre, Middlesex Polytechnic

Pan Books London, Sydney and Auckland

Extracts are reprinted by permission of
Faber and Faber Ltd from *Rites of Passage*
by William Golding

First published 1988 by Pan Books Ltd
Cavaye Place, London SW10 9PG
9 8 7 6 5 4 3 2 1

ISBN 0 330 50265 4
Photoset by Rowland Phototypesetting Ltd
Bury St Edmunds, Suffolk
Printed and bound in Great Britain by
Richard Clay Ltd, Bungay, Suffolk

Contents

Page references are to the Faber edition of *Rites of Passage* but as references are also given to particular chapters, the Notes may be used with any edition of the book.

Preface

The intention throughout this study aid is to stimulate and guide, to encourage the reader's *involvement* in the text, to develop disciplined critical responses and a sure understanding of the main details in the chosen text.

Brodie's Notes provide a summary of the plot of the play or novel followed by act, scene or chapter summaries each of which will have an accompanying critical commentary designed to underline the most important literary and factual details. Textual notes will be explanatory or critical (sometimes both), defining what is difficult or obscure on the one hand, or stressing points of character, style or plot on the other. Revision questions will be set on each act or group of chapters to test the student's careful application to the text of the prescribed book.

The second section of each of these study aids will consist of a critical examination of the author's art. This will cover such major elements as characterization, style, structure, setting, theme(s) or any other aspect of the book which the editor considers needs close study. The paramount aim is to send the student back to the text. Each study aid will include a series of general questions which require a detailed knowledge of the set book; the first of these questions will have notes by the editor of what *might* be included in a written answer. A short list of books considered useful as background reading for the student will be provided at the end.

Graham Handley

The author and his work

It is appropriate that solitude should be a recurring motif in William Golding's novels, for this writer has the public appearance of a deeply private, even aloof man. He has given occasional interviews, unwillingly, it seems; but prefers to keep to himself. In an age when even the most famous novelists fall over themselves to give their views on everything from bedside reading to nuclear war, such privacy is refreshing. It also tells us a good deal about Golding's work and his attitude to the world presented in that work. He is an idiosyncratic writer: experimental, intense, visionary, unafraid to tackle great themes, and to tackle them in an explicitly religious manner (though I shall have more to say about what 'religion' means in this context). As a result, his work can be both thrilling and embarrassing, moving and wooden, by turns; and demands from the reader a concentrated attention to detail, plus the ability to think in large spans, which it requires all Golding's undoubted brilliance as a story-teller to sustain.

Golding was born in 1911 in a small Cornish village, his early childhood coinciding with the First World War. He read English at Brasenose College, Oxford and became a teacher when he graduated in 1933. Six years later he married. In 1940 he joined the navy and witnessed and participated in much action at sea during the Second World War. On leaving the navy in 1945 Golding resumed teaching. He enjoys sailing, and as a recreation taught himself classical Greek.

Like nis near-contemporary, Graham Greene – a novelist who could hardly be more different – Golding began to build the foundations of his craft in childhood by reading the popular classics of the period, notably Henty (1832–1902), author of historical novels for boys, and Ballantyne (1825–1894) whose *Coral Island* was to become the model for *Lord of the Flies* (1954). The adventure story has been a staple of English fiction, ever since Defoe (1660–1731) invented Colonel Jack, Moll Flanders and – most famous of all – Robinson Crusoe (who is mentioned in this novel); and the tradition stretches down through Fielding, Scott, Dickens, Stevenson and Conrad (and a host of others) to the writers of our own day, whose thrillers and spy stories (think of Le Carré and Deighton) are their descendants. As the list of names I have given suggests, there is no clear demarcation between 'serious' and 'popular' where such writing is concerned, and that is an important point when thinking about Golding: definitely a 'high-brow' novelist who has nevertheless learnt the lessons of this tradition and continued to practise them.

However complex or experimental his writing may become – and the verbal texture is sometimes virtually incoherent – he never loses the powerful narrative drive vital to the good novelist. This was evident in his first published novel, *Lord of the Flies*, which came out when Golding was 43, comparatively late in life. The ten volumes of fiction issued since are all very different from one another, but certain common characteristics and themes are already apparent in that book, which tells the story of a group of English schoolboys, stranded on an island, who rapidly degenerate from comparatively civilized behaviour into savagery, worshipping a strange god and sacrificing to it. The sacrificial victim is a common figure in Golding's work – Pangall in *The Spire* (1964) and Colley are notable examples – and he is fascinated by the relationship between the misfit and the group, between civilization and savagery, between reason and instinct. All these themes can be found in *Rites of Passage*. He also returns again and again to religion – presented often enough as a human attempt to acknowledge the mysteries at the heart of existence, which goes disastrously wrong or misses the point.

The comparison with Greene is once again illuminating. A catholic convert of long standing and once a communist, Greene is obsessed by the problem of institutionalizing belief in a way which makes it expressible and productive; but his novels show that the church and the party, however well-meaning, cannot help but repress or pervert individual acts of virtue. At the same time, it seems that only the structure of such institutions can give these acts meaning: that is why, in the end, Greene's characters find themselves compelled to choose even when they know their choices mean misfortune and sometimes destruction. Golding is interested in such matters at what one might call a more basic, even more primitive level: not with this institution or that, but with the very nature of institutionality. A church, a school, a ship's company, a party of children, a tribe, or a whole society – how do they work? How do they come into being and decline? What forces drive them? These are the questions Golding asks, focussing on the critical points of growth or decay, conflict and chaos, where institutions reveal their natures most clearly. Where religion is concerned this means paying attention not to one doctrine or another (though these play a part), nor to the merits of this creed or that; but to the fundamental relationships between church and individual, inexpressible personal vision and communal observance, instinctive urges and social discipline.

All these features appear in Golding's work from *Lord of the Flies* to his latest novel, which is a sequel to *Rites of Passage*, *Close Quarters* (1987). But there is also another feature of his writing already apparent in the first novel which is of primary importance throughout his oeuvre: style. For Golding is not only an idiosyncratic stylist, who delights in varying the normal rhythm and structure of sentences, introducing strange words (as a child, he tells us, he was fascinated by unusual vocabulary), and solving fearsome problems, such as communicating the feelings and thoughts of prehistoric creatures who have no language (in *The Inheritors*); he is also preoccupied by the relationship between style – in the widest sense of the word – and subject. This no doubt has a lot to do with his choice of unusual subjects. Several have already been mentioned, but others include ancient Egypt (*The Scorpion God*), the invention of steam engines in the first century AD (*Envoy Extraordinary*), the last moments of a drowning man's life (*Pincher Martin*) and the adventures of a visionary, deformed child who is born and dies in fire (*Darkness Visible*). Each of these subjects requires different treatment and, while certain features of Golding's style recur, each story has a very different feeling to it. They are united by a visionary intensity, sometimes heightened and sometimes mitigated by a growing interest in comedy. *Rites of Passage* is perhaps his most successful combination so far of the comic and the intense, and one of his most successful stylistic experiments. Once more Greene is a suitable comparison. Having flirted with surrealism in his early days, Greene soon opted for a comparatively plain, traditional style of great flexibility and apparent transparency. The reader has to pay close attention to detect the rhetorical strategies, the metaphors and other stylistic devices at work in his prose; and he has continued to refine it as he has grown older. Golding still has an exuberance lacking in Greene, which sometimes leads him into trouble. In a marvellous novel such as *Darkness Visible* (1979) we find, especially in the conversations, weaknesses Greene would never allow: bathos, miscalculated slang, false notes. On the other hand, the extraordinary beginning of this book in which the central character, Matty, appears to emerge out of a fire, is something Greene could never achieve – nor presumably would ever want to.

Unlike his great contemporary, Golding has taken little part in public affairs, rarely pronouncing on events or even writing to the papers. We therefore have to judge his novels on their merits – which underlines the fact that Golding rarely seems to be making a point. Even when, as in *Rites of Passage*, a clearly deplorable episode occurs, our instinctive condemnation is always balanced against the complexity of things. Blame may be apportioned within the book, but readers should be wary of reaching easy conclusions. Who is guilty of Colley's death? This is *not* the question Golding puts. Instead he asks: are guilt and innocence appropriate categories for us to use? or even, what does it mean to say that someone is guilty or innocent? And if Golding occasionally falls into a kind of sentimental mysticism (as at the end of *Darkness Visible*) this is unimportant in the context of his extraordinary ability to render mystical experience without committing himself to an interpretation of its validity.

Source and Plot

Source

In an interview with James Baker (*Twentieth Century Literature*, vol. 28 no. 2) Golding has given the source of the plot as an incident recorded in an early 19th-century diary. A parson in a convoy to the Philippines wandered, naked and drunk, among the soldiers and sailors, then took to his bed and died. On this fragment Golding builds a short but complex and subtle story, which depends for much of its force not on the events but on the form in which they are narrated.

Plot

The plot can be summed up in a single sentence: a clergyman, bound for Australia, is maltreated by almost everyone aboard the ship, from the captain down, and eventually dies from shame. However, such a summary, though fair enough in one way, would be completely inadequate in another, for it omits the novel's crucial question. To what extent are the others responsible for Colley's death, and to what extent does he have only himself to blame?

Let us consider the plot in more detail. Colley is clearly out of place from the beginning. Not only has the captain's loathing of clergymen been transmitted to his officers and crew: this particular clergyman is shy, awkward, unsophisticated. These qualities in themselves could hardly precipitate his downfall. Under normal circumstances he would simply retire into himself and keep his head down. But there is something about Colley – whether we call it faith or theatricality or a mixture of both is open to question – which drives him on to his fate, forcing him to confront the captain and, even when he has extracted a kind of apology, to push his luck by venturing among the notoriously brutal sailors. This 'something' is further complicated by the fact that Colley is discovered to be homosexual, and it is a drunken homosexual act, soberly remembered, which causes him to will his own death. But sexual shame alone is not enough to explain how the catastrophe occurs; for a different man with similar desires would either have suppressed them or been careful not to expose himself in public.

Bearing all this in mind, we might rewrite the plot summary above as follows:

The Reverend Robert Colley is travelling to Australia aboard a ship whose captain loathes clergymen. Provoked by Colley's attempts to approach him, Captain Anderson actually knocks the man down, and this example proves crucial in demonstrating to the crew that they, too, may mistreat him if they wish. When the ship reaches the Equator he is accordingly singled out for rough treatment in the ceremony of Crossing the Line. Appalled by the insult to his clerical status, as he sees it, Colley demands an apology from the Captain, who grudgingly gives it. He also demands to be allowed access to the crew and lower deck passengers in order to rebuke them. He is warned against this by the Captain and others, but insists. Meanwhile, he has become infatuated with two men: one an upper-class fellow traveller who is distantly polite, and the other a virile, handsome sailor. In order to carry out his mission to the lower decks, he dresses up in all his ecclesiastical finery and goes down there. Once with the sailors, he accepts a glass of rum as a conciliatory gesture and, quite unused to drink, immediately becomes drunk and agrees to accompany them below decks, where he commits an act of fellatio with the handsome sailor. Subsequently appearing on deck drunk, singing and semi-naked, Colley is escorted to his cabin, where he remains, overcome by such shame, that he apparently wills himself to death. A perfunctory inquest is conducted and the captain, determined to conceal the real cause of death, puts it down in his log as a fever.

This elaborated plot indicates far more clearly the complex causes of Colley's downfall and, in particular, his own role in bringing it about. But it still does not give the full facts, for there is another major element in the book which conditions the shape of the plot: the narrative viewpoints. The story is told by two narrators and it is only when we have both accounts that we get a full picture. First there is Talbot's journal, which begins as the detached account of a sophisticated, worldly young man, designed to please his patron and fill in the boring weeks aboard ship. But after Colley's death, Talbot – the young man he admired – finds the clergyman's letter to his sister which gives a detailed account of events from his point of view, up to his preparations for going among the crew. The viewpoint switches dramatically from detached to involved, from exterior to interior, and the new perspective reshapes our view of the plot. But it also has to be said that it complicates the reader's task, in the sense that to provide more explanation is not always to provide more enlightenment. A simple story of Colley's downfall is no longer possible, once we have the two versions of events. We can't blame it only on his conflict with the captain, or only on his naivety, or only on his sexual desires, or only on circumstances; we have to take them all into account. What is a simple plot in terms of action therefore becomes intricate and ambiguous in terms of motivation, meaning, and cause and effect.

Finally we need to consider the impact on the plot of an element apparently unconnected with it: literary allusion. Both Colley and Talbot are men educated in the humanist tradition of classical literature, and they both refer to Greek drama. Talbot is also a novel reader, and makes many allusions to eighteenth-century fiction. The general tendency of Talbot's references is to suggest a complex relationship between life and art. The plots in literary works are closed, complete: we know what has happened and why. But in life, the action is never over and never completely comprehensible. To begin with Talbot views Colley as a kind of play – which means that he, Talbot, can remain a detached spectator. But gradually he is drawn in to the action: the question of moral responsibility arises, and he has to take action. When that happens, it is no longer possible to remain detached, to watch the drama as a member of the audience. And yet – there is a sense in which we always remain spectators, not only of other people's dramas, but also of our own. And this means that what happens is not just a matter of events external to us and to others: it is always conditioned by our response to what has already happened. We are at once participants and audience in our own lives and in the lives of others. Talbot thus comes to see that he is part of the drama he has been observing and narrating – though this does not prevent him from continuing to regard it as a kind of performance. Perhaps the point is that we need to turn things into plot in order to understand them – but once we do that we inevitably begin to dramatize, to falsify and to mystify. At the end of *Rites of Passage*, we are no nearer to the meaning of the plot than we were at the beginning.

Chronology and setting

Chronology

The book is set in the early 19th century, some time towards the end of the Napoleonic Wars. Golding himself has dated the book in 1812 or 1813 (interview with James Baker – see Further Reading). This makes it an historical novel with all the consequences that implies.

To begin with, it is remote enough from us to seem strange and intriguing. At the same time, the themes are timeless. Golding has no truck with those contemporary writers who deny the idea of human nature. His novels, whether set in the prehistoric past or the present, deal with recognizable humanity. Then, the particular period chosen is a significant one, a time of transition between two ages. Though the action of the book is exactly contemporary with the novels of Jane Austen (1775–1817) who belongs very much to the eighteenth century, the living writer most frequently cited is the romantic poet, Coleridge (1772–1834). We are aware of the contrast between two ways of feeling and thinking in the styles of Talbot and Colley. Talbot's narrative begins in a recognizably eighteenth century manner: witty, sophisticated, cool, eminently sensible and worldly. But the experiences of witnessing Colley's downfall and reading his letter effect a subtle change, darkening and enriching Talbot's outlook and thereby his literary style. Colley's style is also recognizably eighteenth century in a different manner: formal, demure, even pompous, but his letter is interspersed with intimations of deeper feeling, and the style accordingly becomes more charged.

The time-sequence within the book is deliberately blurred. Talbot begins with a daily record in his journal, but soon abandons this as he loses track of the days in his attacks of sea-sickness; and then, when Colley's drama develops, begins to think of time in terms of events, not clock measurements. In doing this, Golding makes deliberate reference to eighteenth-century novels which experiment with time, notably *Tristram Shandy* by Sterne, in which the hero discovers that the more he writes about his own life, the more he has to write, as he unearths the causes of events, then the causes of those causes, and the causes of those causes . . . until his narrative begins to go backwards in time. This doesn't happen in *Rites of Passage*, but time does stretch as the book proceeds.

Setting

The story's setting is obviously of vital importance, contributing as much to the development of the plot as any of the human agents. Situated aboard a decaying ship near the end of a long and exhausting war, the novel constantly compares the vessel with the world, complete in itself, and even possessing its own God in the person of Captain Anderson. But a ship is more confined than the world: for the passengers and crew there is no escape from each other – except overboard – and the claustrophobic herding together, even among the grander travellers, noted by Talbot and Colley, is instrumental in promoting the drama, whether it is a matter of Talbot's absurd affair with Zenobia, or Colley's entrapment in his cabin by Deverel and Cumbershum. The difficult atmosphere is made worse by the mood of the Captain and his officers, who know that their days are numbered as the war approaches its end, and who resent being consigned to a fifth-rate vessel.

The decay of the ship – and the stench it gives off – symbolize the decadent moral state into which crew and passengers decline, their isolation from human society allowing the growth of strange fears and fancies, and the practice of violent customs. Colley, in particular, has a vision of the craft's extreme fragility, suspended as it is between sky and sea, miles of water below, miles of space above. The symbolism of life's voyage is as old as literature itself, but here it is given a new twist by the material importance of the ship: smelly, creaking, in urgent need of repairs. Within this precarious domain, certain areas are rigidly marked out: for example the captain's patch, the sailors' quarters, the purser's hidden darkness; and characters stray out of their proper place only at their own risk, as Colley's fate, first at the Captain's hands, and then with the crew, so graphically illustrates. To this extent, the ship does symbolize the world left behind, the world of class distinctions and careful divisions. On the other hand, the penalties paid for transgression are far more violent, in keeping with savage naval discipline, and the morality of human relationships is far less certain. To that extent, the travellers are entering an unknown territory, which symbolizes not the land they have left but the new country they are going to.

This new country constantly hovers in the text, much as the old country does. Though the entire action takes place aboard ship, constant references are made, by both Colley and Talbot, to particular places in England, while both of them contemplate the life that is to come. But in addition to this world, reference is also constantly made to the next: to heaven and to hell. Colley wonders whether he is indeed already in hell, having earlier described the seascape as heavenly, while Talbot, who nominally believes in neither, nevertheless uses the language of devils and gods to describe parts of his experience. Thus we realize that not only are bodies travelling, but also souls: they too are making a journey, both within this world, and from here to whatever there may be of the next. When Colley's body is sent to the bottom of the sea with cannonballs about his feet, we contrast this with the traditional image of the soul rising to heaven, which Colley himself has earlier invoked, and the contrast leaves a question mark. At no time does Golding either dismiss Christianity or confirm it: instead, he leaves the question, like the boat, in a kind of limbo. And that place (or non-place) mentioned by Talbot – a kind of purgatory – is, in a sense, where the action occurs.

Chapter commentaries, textual notes and revision questions

Chapter 1

In this first section we are introduced to one of the two narrators, Edmund Talbot, and to the ship in which he is to travel. Immediately one of the novel's grounding tensions is established – between the would-be superior tone of the writer and his distinctly inferior new environment. Class distinctions are to be a theme of the novel, but these apply to more than social relations: they pervade the whole environment, moral and physical. Thus Talbot begins by adopting the jaunty tone of the refined but manly young gentleman, prepared to treat roughing it as an adventure ('I am determined to speak the tarry language') but only at arm's length. This point is underlined by his constant awareness of, and reference to, the lofty status of his correspondent – who does not need to appear or reply for us to have a very clear picture of a man on whom Talbot clearly models himself: a grand seigneur whose worldly, cynical manner Talbot apes.

The device of the letter is obviously helpful for establishing details of setting and plot, but it is also part of Golding's literary pastiche in a novel which refers back ironically to a number of early nineteenth-century fictional conventions. Talbot is not unlike the hapless narrator of another historical novel set in the same period: Mr Lockwood in *Wuthering Heights*. He, too, is a foppish man of the world who learns less than he thinks he has by the end of the book; and he, too, opens the novel, in a comparably dandified manner. And like Lockwood, Talbot provides an ironic link between the worlds of high fashion and low passion.

Antipodes New Zealand.
Goldsmith . . . Goldsmith (1728–1774), Richardson (1689–1761), Fielding (1707–1754) and Smollett (1721–1771) were eighteenth-century novelists. For a comment on their significance see the section on *Style*.
irons As part of their punishment – and to secure them – convicts were sometimes transported in chains.
wooden walls A popular name for the English Navy – the country's defence against invasion.
The stink A fairly obvious symbol for the moral corruption which pervades the ship.
There's nothing . . . Words which ironically foreshadow Anderson's role in the drama.

Let me describe . . . Detailed descriptions of setting are a familiar feature of English eighteenth-century novels.

good-humouredly Note the tone of self-approval here.

furled Rolled up.

hutch, or sty The references to animals in this paragraph point to the bestial events to come.

mizzen mast Etymologically, this ought to mean the middle mast. In fact, it means the mast nearest the stern in a three-masted ship.

Aft of Behind.

offices of necessity Lavatories.

lying to a hawser Secured with a rope (rather than a chain).

pitched within . . . Talbot contrasts the new, metal-bottomed ships with this elderly wooden craft, anticipating Colley's horror at being separated from the water only by a thin wooden skin.

struck Taken.

Marine Dictionary Published in 1769.

tarry i.e. the language of sailors or tars, so-called from the tarring of sails.

staff and guide The Biblical allusion is one of many in the novel.

Our Noah Anderson is later compared to a hidden, angry god. Even here he is said to be invisible.

the better sort One of the novel's ironies – part of a larger pattern – results from Talbot's mistake about the social class of the officers.

a younger parson The first reference to Colley. 'Parson' is always a somewhat dismissive term for a clergyman.

a bride This ironically anticipates Colley's 'rape' by Billy Rogers.

veer Change direction.

a-weigh A misusage resulting from the confusion between getting 'away' and 'weighing' the anchor.

guns Fired to signal departure.

hell fire The ship is compared to a small world. But the novel also implies that it is a small universe, with a God (Anderson), a heaven (where the upper-class passengers dwell) and a hell (where the ballast is). But heaven and hell are also shown to be states of mind, or temporary experiences.

gimbals Mechanisms for keeping hanging objects level – not working too well, apparently.

Old England This phrase initiates a complex series of references, by comparing England to the stinking ballast – the source of the class-distinctions which are at the root of Colley's catastrophe. The new land of Australia really is new: an unknown land which is potentially heaven or hell.

ladder This conventional use of the metaphor anticipates the role played by some actual ladders later in the story.

ambition Ambition has a role to play in the story. Talbot mistakes Colley's respect for social ambition – a wish to climb the ladder of snobbery.

unworthy An ambiguous usage, considering the obvious worldliness of Talbot's correspondent. Ironically it turns out that his cruel behaviour is indeed worthy of his cynical patron.

Revision questions on Chapter 1

1 What do we learn about Talbot from this first chapter?

2 Is there anything distinctive about the vocabulary?

3 Describe the ship in your own language.

4 What is symbolism? Is there any in this chapter?

Chapter 2

Little happens in this chapter, but a good deal is conveyed – vital in a book where the substance is not action but reflection, not being but knowing. Primarily we are given an account of Talbot's first hours aboard the ship when under way, but at the heart of this description is half a paragraph detailing the first full encounter with Colley. The tone of the letter is light-hearted: Talbot takes care to present himself, even to his godfather, as a laconic man of the world, capable of profound observation, but taking nothing too seriously. The farcical encounter with Colley fits in with this approach – and his appearances continue to be largely comical for much of the book, even when he is being humiliated. It is only gradually that the full import, the blackness of this comedy, sinks in and we reflect back on the clues this early scene gives us about the outcome of the drama: the ominous images of the trapped bird, the drunken crab and the bullying ship; the parson's unsuitable clothes; his lack of physical control. What was farcical – even slapstick – becomes tragic, as the heat and the brilliance of the light increase, and the moral atmosphere darkens.

As in the first chapter, Talbot amuses himself with the 'tarry' language. This is more than a verbal joke. The problem of translation is a persistent theme in Golding. How can we understand a language not our own? The question can be thought of not only in terms of national tongues but also as applying to communication between individuals. Can I ever be sure that I even begin to understand what *you* mean, when I so often experience frustration in communicating to you what *I* mean? As with Colley's tragedy, these questions only emerge gradually out of the novel's comic verbal play, but there is a moment at the end of the chapter when the point is tellingly made. Talbot resolves to be suspicious of Wheeler, but he cannot be sure how suspicious he should be. When Wheeler disappears in mysterious circumstances near the end of the book, we are left with that uncertainty? Did Wheeler try to give Talbot hints about Colley? Did Talbot misunderstand them – or not?

careful composition This is one of many references to writing in both narratives (Talbot's and Colley's). Note how Talbot deliberately sets out to shape the narrative to amuse his patron. He is going to write it like a novel – or perhaps like a play: the text is filled with references to the theatre.

I do not know Notice how the syntax comically mimics Talbot's confusion, brought on by seasickness.

Seneca off Naples Seneca (4 BC–65 AD) taught the doctrine of Stoicism i.e. that one should rise above pain and pleasure in order to avoid their power.

paregoric A soothing medicine containing opium and camphor.

poppy i.e. the opium poppy.

sensibly Noticeably i.e. apparent to the senses.

trivet Tripod.

convocation Gathering. Methodism was relatively new and much despised by Anglicans and sceptics alike as being absurdly melodramatic, uncouth and potentially anarchic.

blow Minor storm.

a chaplain The first hint of Anderson's strange quirk. This point follows ironically after Talbot's condescending words about Methodism.

waist The middle of the ship.

bulwarks The side of the ship projecting above the deck.

ratlines Part of the rigging.

eye of light Golding breaks out of the pseudo eighteenth-century style into a piece of vivid writing.

'have the legs' Can go faster than.

speak Hail.

Ushant An island off the extreme west coast of Brittany where the squadron is on station – presumably because of the war with France. (Now usually called Ile d'Oessant.)

the line i.e. the battle line.

convoyed Because of the war it is necessary for 'civilian' ships to be escorted by a warship beyond the range of the French fleet.

a parson Colley's first full-scale description is appropriately absurd.

heard by no one Ironic in view of what happens – and especially ironic in terms of the ship, where even the Almighty i.e. Anderson, ignores him.

a trapped bird A pathetic image looking forward to Colley's fate.

Of *course*. . . The parenthesis signals Talbot's bad faith: he is showing off (the bird, the crab) to his patron.

on his knees Again anticipating the future – this time the occasion of Colley's disgrace.

heave Talbot's word-play: the ship heaves like its sick passengers.

grabbed him This time Talbot saves him – the next time he fails to do so.

little man The tone is unmistakeably contemptuous.

befouling The physical squalor of faeces, urine and vomit plays an important part in the plot.

For some reason Perhaps because the water relieves Talbot of his contact and therefore of his responsibility. There is an ironic allusion here to the cleansing of baptismal waters. But as we are to discover, it is inward foulness, which cannot be simply washed away, that counts.

lees Remains – as at the bottom of a wine bottle.

shrouds Ropes linking the masts to the side.

mainbrace The brace on the mainyard, which is the cross-beam on the mast over which the sail is stretched. The mainyard is on the main mast.

Comprehension This moment of understanding the ship looks forward to more significant moments of moral understanding later in the book. These are like instants of visionary illumination.

a what? Just as Talbot perceives a ship as more than a collection of ingenious mechanisms, so he later has a gleam of insight into the possibility that this may be true of human beings also.

a means . . . As the book progresses we begin to understand this phrase as a question. We can see how a ship works to an end – but what about the world? If, like Talbot, we are unbelievers, does not life appear purposeless? Does Colley, for all his absurdity, have access to a deeper understanding than the suave Talbot?

complacency This acknowledgement only serves to underline the fact that Talbot is a good deal more – and more dangerously – complacent than he knows.

first harmonic Talbot obligingly explains the meaning of this term in the following phrase. Its significance here is the connection with the ancient philosophical doctrine associated with Pythagoras (580–500 BC) who explains the structure of the universe in terms of harmony and discord. Here Talbot implies that all is harmonious i.e. that the world is a very satisfactory place where everything fits. Clearly, this is not the case for men such as Colley or Anderson. Images of concord and discord, wholeness and fragmentation play an important part in the text. In the following lines ('a ferocious music' etc.) Talbot shows some inkling of darker times.

a drunken angle The notion of things out of their true angle frequently recurs.

the purser The beginning of a running joke about the purser. It eventually transpires that all the officers are in debt to him.

to see round and through him This, of course, is precisely what Talbot fails to do with Colley. At stake here is not only knowledge of others, but also self-knowledge.

interesting events . . . Talbot is wrong – but the interest turns out to be something very different to his expectations.

Revision questions on Chapter 2

1 Comment on Colley's first appearance.

2 What do we learn about Talbot from his description of Colley?

3 Identify the metaphors in this chapter and say what part they play.

4 'a means working to an end . . .' What significance does this phrase have in relation to the novel as a whole?

Chapter 3

Talbot has his first encounter with one of the officers, the coarse Mr Cumbershum, who gives him a number of clues about the nature of life aboard the ship. Clearly all is not well. Cumbershum is dubious when Talbot, somewhat satirically, describes the officers as 'devoted', and he makes it clear that the captain is a man of strong views, a propos their discussion concerning the parson. Notice how positively Golding is preparing the ground for Colley's drama, featuring some aspect of him in almost every chapter, gradually building up a picture before we hear from the man himself. The style of broad comedy with dark undertones is continued.

fouler liquids Excrement. The sense of this pervades the book, climaxing in the badger-bag scene.
she lurched The book constantly compares the ship to a small world. But it is an insecure, unfamiliar world, in which the inhabitants are compelled to find new ways of behaving.
necessary objects This new behaviour involves the recognition that familiar things can become strange – not be what one thought they were.
genii . . . Native spirits. Dryads were supposed to inhabit woods; hamadryads lived and died with the trees they inhabited.
on all fours So Talbot is in just as undignified a position as Colley. He shares the same human frailty in this respect. Is he *morally* comparable? This is the question the book asks us.
transverse . . . bulkhead A bulkhead separates one part of the ship from another. The transverse bulkhead goes across the ship.
clownish Talbot persists in seeing others as more clownish than himself.
'rigging screws' Fastenings for the ropes supporting masts and sails.
accounted a gentleman A crude example of Talbot's snobbery. Officers and ranks, then as now, usually came from different classes.
the most inept . . . This is a sign of poor naval pay in general, the dangers of the service, and the particular reputation of this ship.
Mumbo Jumbo Nonsense. This reference characterizes Talbot's attitude to religion which he sees merely as a necessary support for the powers of the state.
Captain Cook The great explorer who discovered Australia.

other business It is not yet made clear what this is.
philosophy Calmness.
roast Tease.
turned the thing off Took it in good part.
passe-partout Passport.
'go about' Do something different.
bosky Tipsy.
small ale Ale with little malt in.
tarpaulins Sailors.

Revision questions on Chapter 3

1 What role does weather play in the novel?

2 Describe Cumbershum. What is the purpose of his conversation with Talbot?

3 Do we learn anything about Captain Anderson?

Chapter 4

Talbot visits the Captain on deck, and Golding begins to bring out the ambivalence of the young man's position. In many ways this will only become clear when we read Colley's narrative, but certain aspects of it are already apparent. In particular, there is the strange power-relationship between the two men. Anderson is almost literally the god of the ship: his authority is absolute and he has powers over life and death. But he is overawed by the authority of Talbot's patron, and on page 31 we can observe, through Talbot's eyes, the struggle within the Captain between angry assertion of his predominance and acknowledgement of a higher power. But although he does not yet realize it, this also puts Talbot, amused at the Captain's reaction, in a potentially awkward position, for here he is flouting a duly constituted authority, while himself claiming to stand for the idea of authority in general. Although he sees himself as a representative of the state's power, he enjoys the anarchic feeling of undermining its embodiment in Anderson. This points to the complexity of a class system which is built on power relations of an arbitrary kind, always likely to be undermined as interest dictates. Only when he is asked to sit on the board of enquiry into Colley's death does his predicament become apparent.

shoulderings Shudderings.
drag Brake.
the damned Another reference to hell.
aria Song in an opera. This is one of many references to the theatre (see section on imagery).
sheets Sails.
yards The beams on the masts.
forrard . . . quarter! i.e. They had changed the sails to take more of the wind.
ample i.e. the ship rises and falls in the water, but now with less strain.
Mistress *Pamela* Richardson's novel *Pamela* (1740), already alluded to on p.3, concerns a maidservant's resistance of her master's attempt at seduction, and her eventual marriage to him. Readers still argue about whether her virtue is principled or a devious way of achieving a marriage above her station. The allusion follows the previous paragraph's reference to the ship as a woman, reflecting ironically on Talbot's own situation: like Pamela's 'master' he is at the mercy of his 'servant' – the ship.
in a single sentence A further reference to Richardson's novel, in which the literary style is both minutely detailed and meant to record events almost as they happen.
to choose what I say Yet another reference to Richardson, whose novels are exceptionally long. Writing is becoming a kind of addiction for Talbot, as it is for Richardson's characters.
beaver A fur hat. Note the potential absurdity of his appearance – not so different to Colley.
ignored my greeting Talbot misreads the situation, as does Colley later. It is not rudeness which motivates Cumbershum here, but fear of the Captain.
astonished . . . strike me Compare Colley's meetings with the Captain.
atrabilious Melancholy.
the humours According to the theory of humours, the world is composed of four elements: earth, air, fire and water. Human character is determined by the proportion of these elements, and the humours they generate, in its make-up.
Grande Porte Turkish Imperial Government – named after the site of its offices (the gate or porte).
Arras room Arras is tapestry. The reference is to a room in his lordship's house.
ordnance Artillery.
driver A large sail stretching over the stern.
gentling Soothing.
sufficient force Talbot returns to this idea.
intolerable . . . But this is what Anderson does do to Colley.

Revision questions on Chapter 4

1 Explain the reference to Mistress Pamela.

2 What is the significance of Anderson's changing attitude to Talbot?

3 Describe the style of Talbot's writing in this chapter.

Chapter 5

This section describes another encounter with Colley, apparently as a minor episode in a chapter devoted to Talbot's exploration of the ship. In fact the two are connected, for the substance of the chapter is the detailed description of a rite – shooting the sun – and the reactions of its observers. This anticipates – though we do not know it – another series of rites: the humiliation and destruction of Colley. Compare Colley's reception by Captain Anderson with Talbot's, only a few pages earlier, and the connection becomes apparent. Talbot is master of the situation, but Colley is already a victim, a spectacle – a spectacle, moreover, which has been anticipated by Cumbershum and Taylor. The interview does indeed result in Colley's destruction – not instantly but eventually, because the captain's behaviour makes it safe for Colley's tormentors to bully him.

fourth . . . fifth A small point, but the beginning of a confusion which rapidly deepens as the voyage progresses. Uncertainty about time becomes symbolic of a deeper moral uncertainty.
midshipman A trainee officer – so-called from his quarters amidships.
ancients 'Ancient' is a corruption of 'ensign', and there may be a reference to Iago (in *Othello*), who was refused promotion.
in pious hope i.e. because there was nothing gentlemanly about him. Once again Talbot's patronizing manner is apparent.
Sacred Precincts One of Talbot's persistent references to Anderson as a god.
votary One devoted by a vow.
boom Pole across which a sail is stretched.
white line Line divided the first-class passengers from the rest, who were not allowed to cross it.
capstan An implement for winding cable e.g. the anchor chain.
bowsprit A spar projecting over the ship's bows.
επ ενρεα νωτα θαλασσης 'on the broad southern oceans.' The phrase is Homer's.
impertinence Talbot's distaste does not suggest to him that the men may dislike *him* looking down on *them*.
French The quotation is in Greek, of course, which gives Talbot a further excuse to feel superior. But he has no business to suppose that such a boy will know Greek, and the feeling reflects badly on Talbot himself.

shoot the sun Take bearings from the sun.
Articles of War The rules governing the conduct of hostilities.
sweeten Talbot making fun of Willis.
his father gave him Cadets were expected to equip themselves.
sextant An instrument with an arc the sixth of a circle (from the Latin *sextans*: six) used for calculating altitudes.
navigation Establishing a position.
Ptolemy Ptolemaic theory, replaced by Copernicus, held that the sun revolved round the earth. Talbot persists in teasing Willis, but Willis's own dim literalism puts the joke on Talbot himself.
'Eppur si muove?' 'Behold it moves.' Galileo's words when demonstrating the earth moves round the sun, not vice versa. This was first shown by Copernicus (1473–1543). Kepler (1571–1630) discovered elliptical orbits.
rite This, too, is one of the rites of passage.
a respect . . . service In marked contrast to their behaviour during the rite of Colley's humiliation. But this respect is just as irrational as that cruelty.
Mumbo Jumbo Having come to mean any incomprehensible nonsense, this was the garbled name of a West African god. Hence the reference to clay feet.
hist Hush.
follies of democracy In this period the vote was still restricted to a small number of people, but elections were dominated by popular opinion. In France, however, the Revolution had taken place about 20 years before the time of this story – presumably the object of Talbot's aristocratic contempt.
such concepts Duty, privilege and authority are central themes of the book. Here Talbot complacently sees in the scene what he wants to see i.e. a reverential proletariat (the sailors) respectfully observing the mysteries of authority (represented by the rite of shooting the sun). Later in the book, we are invited to consider whether such other rites as the sacrifice of Colley are not equally necessary to the maintenance of social hierarchy and order.
How noble . . . Appropriately, Talbot's discovery of the necessity of preserving the status quo is followed by an absurdly pompous lyrical passage, even more absurdly cut short by an etc. as Talbot recognizes the conventionality of his words.
devoted . . . The relationship between Willis and Taylor echoes Colley's admiration for Talbot and Talbot's contempt for Colley.
of *course*, one Mr Prettiman The emphasis on this phrase suggests that Talbot's other commission (hinted at on page 23) is to observe the dangerous freethinker Prettiman.
snorter Slang. Someone outstandingly impressive.
incognita Unknown (Latin).
the parson . . . destruction Another lengthy description of Colley. Talbot's physical distaste is evident.
keel-hauled Literally: hauling under the ship's keel from one side to the

other on a rope. The term has come to mean a serious rebuke but in this period it was also still used literally. Naval punishments were severe in the extreme.

Mr Taylor Taylor's reaction anticipates Colley's fate.

per diem Each day.

extreme unction A pun with two meanings: the last rites offered to a dying man; exceptional obsequiousness.

countenance . . . Compare the descriptions of Colley and Anderson (page 31).

comic This is how Talbot still sees it. At the same time, he shows a sense of both gentlemanly dignity and – more important – what he calls common humanity.

so readily Wheeler knows how to ingratiate himself with the important: Talbot and the Captain.

a gentleman ashore The reference is probably to Adam Smith's *Wealth of Nations* (1776), the book which effectively founded the science of political economy. Wheeler alludes to the principle of supply and demand.

furor scribendi The passion for writing (Latin).

Revision questions on Chapter 5

1 Why is Willis introduced? What do we learn from his conversation with Talbot?

2 What is shooting the sun? Why is the ceremony described in such detail?

3 What is Talbot's attitude to Colley's embarrassment?

4 What does Talbot mean by the word 'gentleman'?

5 What is *furor scribendi*, and what significance does the phrase have in this context?

Chapter X

Talbot now describes the first meeting of all the superior passengers in an episode which contrives to distinguish individuals while hinting at the sense of the mob they potentially make up. While Talbot takes – and expects to take – the leading role in the company as its most socially prominent member, he nevertheless finds that he, too, is part of the crowd, however much he may stand aloof: he makes mistakes, becomes involved in embarrassing moments. Although he is 'properly announced' – as though at a Society party (page 46) – he finds himself in a most undistinguished company, whose behaviour deteriorates with drink and rowdiness (page 53). Despite the social comedy, the scene has violent undertones in the argument between Prettiman and Brocklebank, the vulgar laughter of the crowd, the bad language, the noise, the embarrassing misunderstanding and the powerful current of sexuality which swirls round Zenobia who, as what Talbot calls 'the only tolerable female object' in the party, flirts outrageously and stirs up the passions of the men. Then there is the unease suggested by Talbot's discovery that the officers hardly know one another or their captain, and are probably unhappy with their commissions.

'X' Talbot is now thoroughly confused about time. This is reflected in his narrative. Just as long periods of time vanish and short ones expand, so the story concentrates on some incidents and ignores other aspects of the journey.

packets and company ships Packet-ships operate regularly between one port and another, carrying 'cargoes' of passengers. Company ships are commercial non-military vessels.

afforded Granted. The term suggests that the captain regards his passengers as a nuisance, not as the object of his trip.

ambush A deliberate but provocative concealment.

Quakerish The Quakers are a religious sect who cultivate extreme simplicity of dress and manners.

A young lady . . . Miss Granham's conversation reveals her former employment.

parti Fiancé.

denotation . . . connotation Meaning . . . association. This incident, like the conversation with Willis, highlights the persistent themes of translation and communication.

gin Trap.

'the discernment of spirits' Delicate perception of souls.

Old Dobbie Talbot wades deeper into embarrassment with this patronizing reference.

turn Plan, or outline.

patronized The painter means commissioned but, in view of Talbot's blunders, we are aware of the word's other sense.

dextrous Talbot's complacency is indeed fatuous. He manages to insult Summers, just as he insulted Miss Granham.

perceptive government The conversation between Talbot and Deverel makes the ship/world comparison explicit.

an unwound clock Hopes of rapid promotion depend on the continuation of the war. But the image suggests that Deverel regards war as the normal state of affairs and peace as the useless clock.

consom Consommé – French for clear soup. Zenobia's use of inaccurate French reveals both her pretentiousness and her vulgarity.

a shout of laughter The crudeness of behaviour foreshadows the crowd violence of Colley's immersion.

scurvy politician The phrase is William Cobbett's (1762–1835) journalist, historian and travel writer.
Lutheran Bible Translation by Martin Luther (1483–1546) the founder of Protestantism.
Dr Johnson Writer and critic and compiler of the first comprehensive dictionary of the English Language (1709–1784).
ambiance Atmosphere.
a performer Here the theatrical metaphor which pervades the book is elaborated in some detail for the first time.
to touch wood The discussion of superstition, apparently inconsequential, anticipates Colley's fate, which results from a superstitious rite involved in crossing the line. The theme is taken up in references to Coleridge's poem *The Ancient Mariner*, on page 59.
Mr Coleridge The poet Samuel Taylor Coleridge (1772–1834) whose *Ancient Mariner* appeared in 1798 in *Lyrical Ballads*, written jointly with William Wordsworth (1770–1850), both being important Romantic poets.
it came to nothing A sly reference to Coleridge's notorious inability to finish any project.
an albatross The event which creates the drama in Coleridge's poem.
pour passer le temps To pass the time. Talbot has observed her use of French.

Revision questions on Chapter X

1 Describe the character of Miss Granham and account for her attitude to Talbot.

2 What mistakes does Talbot make in this chapter and why?

3 Why is the entrance of Zenobia described in this way?

4 Compare the characters of Brocklebank and Prettiman.

5 In what ways is the plot advanced in this chapter?

Chapter 12

The theatrical metaphor so important to the book is explicitly developed in this chapter on two levels. On one, Talbot amuses himself by despising the religious ceremony he himself has made possible, focussing his contempt on the costume and manners of Zenobia and Colley, who seem linked by their absurd extravagance. They are both putting on a performance, which Talbot takes to be – in both cases – not only religious but sexual. Yet on another level the chapter also offers a critique of Talbot himself, for he too is playing a role. When he contemptuously refers to Colley confusing him with the Almighty (page 68) he forgets that he has made the service possible – and has to that extent acted in a God-like role, for no-one else would have prevailed against Captain Anderson. So Talbot really is acting God – a point confirmed by the tone of his reflections, as he appears in his own narrative to look down on lesser mortals with an amused condescension. But the chapter ends on a weary note, for this God is tired of his own creation; he is sour for reasons beyond his understanding, disturbed perhaps by the presence of the truly devout lower orders, and by the sexuality of the eye contact between Colley and Zenobia. Altogether, the mixture of emotions in the scene – religious, sexual, snobbish, cynical – is by no means pleasant.

Bessie i.e. the cow referred to in the previous chapter.
Lord Nelson The great naval hero of the period, killed at the Battle of Trafalgar (1805) and reputed to suffer from sea-sickness.
La Belle Talbot humorously copies Zenobia's French – but this phrase also suggests something sexually provocative and available about her.
conduct a service By encouraging him to do this Talbot is ultimately responsible for Colley's downfall.
Magdalene A prostitute (after New Testament, Luke, 8,2).
pinchbeck Sham.
a shoddy example Talbot's class prejudices are here mingled with his dislike of Established Religion to involve him in a contradiction: an insistence on the importance of hierarchy and a reaction against ecclesiastical authority.
Aristotle Greek philosopher.
that order Colley's appearance appears to confirm Talbot's social views.
fine writing There is a relationship, as Talbot unconsciously perceives, between his literary style and his political opinions.
hedge theatres Open air theatres. Talbot has observed Zenobia and Colley playing parts, but as the previous reference to fine writing shows, he, too, has taken up a role, from the very beginning of the trip. He is, as it were, pretending to be what he is: a man of the world – the point being that his character is no more 'natural' or ordained by providence than any of the others.
actrice Actress (French).
maison d'occasion Brothel.

Revision questions on Chapter 12

1 Lord Nelson is mentioned several times in the book. Why, and with what effect?

2 What do we learn about Talbot and Colley from their first meeting?

3 What is Tarpaulin language?

4 What is 'Aristotle's dictum' and what significance does it have in the novel?

5 Discuss the use of theatrical imagery here and throughout the book.

Chapter 17

A brief cry of pain in which the would-be god becomes all too conscious of his squalid humanity. The moral squalor, sensed in the previous scene, is here matched by physical degradation.

Revision question on Chapter 17

1 What is the significance of this chapter's brevity?

Chapter ?

The irrationalism of Prettiman's rational philosophy, patronized in the last paragraph of this chapter, is not too far from Talbot's own rapidly degenerating state, the result of sea-sickness, paregoric and deepening moral confusion. The dream of Colley suggests the strengthening link between the two men, in spite of Talbot's distaste. Colley is on the way to becoming Talbot's doppelganger or ghostly double, a haunting parody of his own inadequacies. The opium-induced dream reminds us that such dreams were part of literary fashion at the time: De Quincey and Coleridge both gave accounts of them, and dream-visions were part of the Romantic mythology to which Talbot makes allusion in the book.

Mr Sterne Laurence Sterne (1713–1768) author of *Tristram Shandy* (1760), a novel in which every kind of formal and typographical experiment is tried – including some imitated by Golding, such as misnumbering and the use of short chapters.

blunderbuss A handgun with a wide bore.

Revision questions on Chapter ?

1 Who was Sterne? Why is he referred to?

2 Explain the allusion to an albatross.

3 What later significance are Talbot's words 'I am at prayer' to have?

Chapter 23

Talbot's interest in the technicalities of the ship can be set against his increasing immersion in dreams and uncertainties. Calculations and mechanics seem to have a clear-cut certainty about them which is a relief from the moral and social muddle aboard ship.

Revision questions on Chapter 23

1 Why is Talbot so keen to surprise Summers?

Chapter 27

Talbot embarks on an affair with Zenobia, despite his disdain for her and Colley in an earlier chapter, and despite his realization that she is probably a prostitute. After the premonitions of group violence in Chapter X and Captain Anderson's brutal behaviour to Colley in Chapter 5, this is the first clear sign that Talbot himself is affected by the general madness which is to culminate in Colley's degradation.

Can . . . humidity— The petulance of the question points to Talbot's growing confusion, and the style of this chapter confirms a change in his attitudes. To begin with he wrote in a recognizably eighteenth-century style: consciously elegant and relaxed, witty, pedantic, detached, but with elements of something else breaking through. But now that pose – the man of the world recording the world's follies and his own – has begun to break down. Talbot's style becomes livelier, cruder, more colloquial as his tone becomes more feverish, and the urgency of desire breaks through the mannered surface. In the last chapter he referred to Sterne, who takes the speaking style to its limits. In this chapter Talbot abandons arch formality in favour of something more Sternian.

the profession The saucy reference here is to the profession of prostitution.

Martial Roman poet (c40–c104), celebrated for his epigrams.

Theocritus Sicilian poet (3rd century BC).

τον Πανα δεδοιχαμες 'The fear of Pan.'

Pan Pan was the Greek god of pastures, forests, flocks and herds. The word panic is derived from the god's name as he was reputed to be the cause of frightening sounds.
mal de mer Sea sickness.
holy, or indecent Talbot might well apply this coupling to Colley.
temporary madness It is precisely this which afflicts everyone aboard. Having despised Colley and Zenobia, Talbot now finds himself possessed by desire for her.

Revision questions on Chapter 27

1 What do the broken sentences on the first page suggest?

2 Describe Talbot's mood in this chapter.

Chapter 30

In an attempt to find a place for his assignation with Zenobia, Talbot goes to the gun room to talk to the sailors. The contrast is marked between their realistic approach to sex in particular, and life in general, and Talbot's attempts to remain gentlemanly, though in the grip of his desires.

badger bag This turns out to be the pool of excrement Colley is forced to swim in.
'We never saw him again.' Hawthorne's fate anticipates Wheeler's.
doggie Penis. The sailors' ribald conversation strikes a healthy note after the feverish behaviour of the passengers.
commerce Sexual intercourse. Talbot is already trying to find a place for his own meeting with Zenobia.
ordinary Harbour.
careen Turn the ship over on its side to clean it.
a vast head If Anderson is a God on deck, the purser is the ruling divinity below. It is not yet clear when he is heavenly or infernal.
lictor The officer who attended a Roman magistrate.

Revision questions on Chapter 30

1 How is the gun-room contrasted with other areas of the ship?

2 What is the point of the carpenter's story?

3 What is the significance of the bilge, so often referred to?

Chapter Y

Talbot achieves his desire for sexual intercourse – it could hardly be called love – with Zenobia, and immediately feels a revulsion which he expresses through irony, making a private joke of the occasion. But to some extent the joke is on him, for he really is the sort of man he enjoys making fun of. This is subtly suggested by the prose style. Sometimes he speaks in a deliberately theatrical manner; at others he naturally falls into such a manner. 'I favoured her with a light salute, then leapt back into my cabin.' In such a sentence it is impossible to tell whether Talbot is making fun of himself or not. Neither we, nor Talbot himself, can tell where reality ends and acting begins.

While Zenobia and Talbot are engaged in their pleasure in his cabin an 'entertainment' is progressing on deck. It is only later that we learn what form this takes, and what role Mr Prettiman's firing of his gun, which interrupts Talbot and Zenobia at the critical moment, plays in it.

one . . . victories! i.e. his conquest of Lady Hamilton.

My sword . . . Typically, Talbot falls into the language of gallantry at such a moment – which indicates his attempt to detach himself from his own embarrassing behaviour.

Moll **. . . both** The list of books is meant to suggest an absurd muddle. *Moll Flanders* (1722) is a novel about a woman of loose morals by Defoe. *Gil Blas* translated by Le Sage (1781), is a comic parody of knightly deeds. Hervey's book (1755), on the other hand, is a sombre commentary on mortality and the frailty of the flesh.

tops'ls Topsails. The image of 'striking the topsails' fits in with Talbot's facetious metaphors of naval battle to describe his 'engagement' (another image) with Zenobia.

fired Inflamed.

main course A pun on (a) central dish in a meal, (b) the principle direction of a ship, (c) the climax of sexual intercourse.

arms Another pun: (a) weapons, (b) arms. The language in this paragraph and the one following is a pastiche of contemporary literary language and the vocabulary of innuendo among what Talbot would call 'gentlemen'.

debellare . . . subjectis! 'To subdue the proud and spare the conquered!' (Virgil: *Aeneid*)

Venus . . . Lucina! Venus is the goddess of love, Lucina of childbirth in Roman mythology.

explosion This passage recalls the opening of a novel cited earlier, *Tristram Shandy*, in which the hero is conceived while his father's mind is on something else.

Mr Prettiman The coincidence of Mr Prettiman's irrational rationality (page 73) and Talbot's irrational desire, is ironically appropriate. Both are as absurd as Zenobia's affectation of girlishness.

Mr Coleridge Coleridge's poem *The Ancient Mariner* turns on the shooting of an albatross, an action said in the poem to be unlucky.

rowdily successful Ironically, this phrase and the words following could be applied to Talbot and Zenobia.

'You will not desert me?' This conventional melodramatic language shows (a) the banality of Zenobia's mind and (b) how right Talbot is to expect her to be alarmed about the consequences of what they have done.

act three Talbot is half embarrassed and half relishing his part.

Miss Brocklebank He keeps her firmly at a distance.

Aristotelian sadness A reference to the phrase *Post coitum homo tristis est:* Man is sad after intercourse.

her sense of theatre But his sense of theatre could be said to betray him into cynicism.

carnival mask A hint at what is to come. During Colley's humiliation the participants are not their usual selves. But do their physical disguises reveal moral natures while concealing faces? The book implies that this is the case.

père et mère Father and mother. Now it is Talbot's turn to use affected French.

I . . . Brocklebank Talbot enjoys the superiority of knowing the hidden reference to his love-making.

Aristotle This Greek philosopher plays quite a part in Talbot's thinking. Appropriately he is often thought of as conservative.

Revision questions on Chapter Y

1 List the literary allusions and comment on their significance.

2 What different styles are employed in this chapter and why?

3 What are Talbot's feelings towards Zenobia?

Chapter ZETA

This brief chapter contains no action but a moment of reflection in the stage metaphor which has already begun to play such an important part in the novel. Here Talbot, presumably unconsciously, uses it to ease himself into a solution of his problem. Why should not Zenobia – who may turn out to be carrying his child – be married off to Colley? They are, after all, both actors in their way. The comparison Talbot establishes between the church and the stage is linked with the comparison already made between the ship and the world. Stage and church are both places where illusion and reality meet, where our understanding of what the world (or the ship) really is comes under stress.

zeta Greek letter z.
methodistical Talbot sees the Established (Anglican) Church as a prop for authority. The methodist movement which attempted to reform that church in the 18th-century, then broke away from it, was a threat because of its religious intensity and stress on the ultimate authority of the individual conscience.
iron ring i.e. which holds the canvas basin in place.
a break down stage right! Talbot invokes more technical jargon, this time from the theatre.
Beatrice and Benedict The hero and heroine of Shakespeare's *Much Ado About Nothing*, from which the subsequent quotations and allusions are taken.
three bells . . . watch A bell is sounded every half hour. Three bells means one and a half hours have passed.

Revision questions on Chapter ZETA

1 What is the Shakespearian concept?

2 What part does Methodism play in the book?

3 What significance does the reference to Beatrice and Benedict have?

Chapter Z

Walking round the deck, Talbot encounters Colley, who seems to have acquired more dignity. He then finds Colley, to his amazement, confronting the Captain and thanking Summers for firing Mr Prettiman's gun. But when he accosts Colley he is disgusted again by the man's obsequiousness. Zenobia then tells Talbot she has lost a love-letter which he finds in his cabin and returns to her, as baffled by the note and its reappearance as he is by Colley's behaviour and Summers' firing of the gun.

The scene is mainly remarkable for its complication of the plot through a series of theatrical encounters which suggest that nothing is what it seems.

Zed . . . There is no reason why Talbot should not know what day it is, but it seems he is becoming as theatrical as Zenobia. His writing is to him what performance is to her.

stricture Headache.
procure Obtain – but there is also a pun on the notion of obtaining sexual services: procuring.
Van Diemen's Land Northern Australia.
France A reference to the Revolution of 1789, carried through in the name of Reason. Talbot's irony issues from the fact that conservatives considered the Revolution far from reasonable.
our people The sailors.
Versailles The seat of French government and monarchy before the Revolution, and synonymous with elaborate courtesy.
mug Talbot deliberately uses slang here to make fun of Colley's dignity.
Mr Talbot . . . Colley is overcome.
blamed for . . . Talbot is going to say 'blamed for the effect I have on Colley' – but at this moment he cannot know how terribly true that is going to be when Colley meets his fate.
Something had happened It begins to dawn on Talbot that something is wrong.
Delicious Enemy! i.e. woman – described as an Enemy because of the Biblical association with Eve's temptation of Adam.
discharged . . . anyone! There is an ironic contrast here with the consequences of Talbot's sexual frolic which may end by injuring both him and Zenobia.
the Sex A coy eighteenth-century phrase for 'women'.
Mr Talbot . . . at once The whole of this passage down to the bottom of page 100 is a comic parody of melodrama – conscious on Talbot's part, perhaps less so for Zenobia (though she, too, is playing a role, albeit more seriously).
YOUR SAILOR HERO Note the poor spelling in this letter, which gives a clue to its source. Note also its absurd theatrical style, which suggests that the writer is either as foolish as Zenobia or has judged her character well.
Emmas A reference to Lady Hamilton, Nelson's mistress.
I must amuse myself Once again Talbot is playing God.
Plato was right! The reference is to the Greek philosopher who criticized the theatre (notably in *The Republic*) on the grounds that acting a part, or watching a performance, can so confuse one about reality, that it is morally disorientating: pretend to be a wicked man and you may become one.

Revision questions on Chapter Z

1 How does Talbot's attitude to Colley change in this chapter?

2 What role does Summers play?

3 Comment on the style and spelling of Zenobia's note.

4 What does Talbot mean by his reference to Plato?

Chapter Ω

What Talbot conjectures to be, in the opening lines of the chapter, the last scene, is far from being so. Colley appears on deck dressed in all his ecclesiastical costume and proceeds to the fo'castle, where most of the ship's company are gathered. Returning to his cabin, Talbot hears applause and then the distant sound of Colley's voice, and then more applause. Leaving his cabin to see what is happening, he meets Deverel, who begins to discuss Zenobia. Meanwhile the afterdeck fills with 'ladies and gentlemen' who have heard that something is afoot. The noise from the fo'castle increases. While Summers is talking to the captain, two figures emerge dressed in parts of Colley's finery. Tommy Taylor appears to say that Colley is drunk, and Talbot finds he is surrounded by a huge, silent, expectant audience. At this point the drunken Colley emerges, semi-naked, singing. A sailor is deputed to escort him to his cabin, but before going down he urinates in front of the crowd, then blesses them. Captain Anderson seems positively animated by this scene, but Talbot, though he first begins to laugh, changes his mind and is alarmed.

This is the most dramatic scene in Talbot's narrative and the climax of the book's first part, providing the motivation for the rest of the action. It is also the most sustained piece of narrative so far and, as it were, the embodiment of Talbot's obsessive theatrical references. Here is a piece of theatre, indeed, which makes Talbot question his former idea of what drama is and seems to put the very social fabric of the ship under threat. This is no mere amusement, but a serious matter – a piece of play-acting which changes reality. Talbot's problem is what to make of it – and here again the scene completes a theme which has been surfacing intermittently throughout the text. How do we translate the signs we see in the world into a comprehensible language? How do we read faces, interpret technical languages, understand other peoples's feelings and motives? More and more Talbot is driven to ask himself these questions – driven to it by the unexpected testing of his reality consequent on Colley's drama.

omega The last letter of the Greek alphabet; also a symbol of finality.
Deus ex Machina! A god from the machine (Latin). The phrase is a theatrical one referring to the idea of a divinity appearing from the wings at the last minute to sort out the tangles of the plot.
Racine French playwright (1639–99) whose works Talbot's patron is supposed to have translated into English.
the Greeks The tragedians Aeschylus (525–455 BC), Sophocles (496–406

BC) and Euripides (484–406 BC) and the comedian Aristophanes (c. 445–c. 385 BC). These are the founding classic playwrights of Western theatre. Talbot would have read them at school.

Furies The avenging spirits who pursue evil-doers.

billet Note (French). Invariably applied to a love letter.

ecclesiastical finery This is Colley at the height of theatricality.

natural authority . . . Talbot makes a crucial distinction between innate character and acquired role. It is just this distinction which is questioned in the novel.

Church . . . State Emphasizing that the ship is indeed a little world.

Platonic Idea Plato held that the visible world is merely the representation of Divine Forms or Ideas, much as a painting is an imitation of the visible world.

warm Sensuous. Talbot refers to his encounter with Zenobia.

aria In classical operas all the action stops while the singer of an aria expresses one emotion or idea.

Fantalini Presumably Golding's invention.

***social* ears** Social instinct or knowledge.

Sheldonian The university theatre in Oxford.

full fig Full dress.

enthusiasm Enthusiasm, much despised in conventional religious circles, characterized methodism. It involved a kind of emotional, even hysterical abandonment to a sense of sin in more extreme manifestations; but usually signifies mere lack of restraint.

an acrobat The theatrical image has now transferred to the circus.

barbaric finery Barbaric because enthusiastic. Eighteenth-century Anglicanism was keen on decorum.

the whole vessel The entire ship has become a kind of theatre and therefore a source of mystification and illusion.

your lordship's favourite i.e. Racine.

mine Shakespeare.

gaiety Anderson is enjoying the prospect of Colley's humiliation.

plasterer's board Mortar board.

Two figures They have Colley's clothes. At this point we become aware of the stage's critical, even anarchic power, for, as Talbot remarks, the performance is directed at 'their betters'.

tippet Hood.

social stability A euphemism for subordination.

Gallic Race i.e. the French. Talbot refers to the Revolution, which stirred up democracy all over Europe. He equates this with the anarchy and potential mutiny he senses aboard the ship.

Leviathan A huge water animal mentioned in the Bible – Job, 41. By analogy: Satan (also known as the Enemy i.e. of Man).

masthead Punish by sending to the top of the mast.

Billy Boy A song which already has a salacious double meaning, this turns out to refer to Billy Rogers, the sailor with whom Colley disgraces himself.

warm . . . country matters . . . Both phrases suggest sexual frankness. In

retrospect it seems that Colley 'knew' what he was doing while drunk.
rounded . . . event Taken as far as it could go.
Polyphemus One-eyed giant mentioned in the *Odyssey of Homer*.
évanouissement Fainting (French).

Revision questions on Chapter Ω

1 Explain and comment on Talbot's allusion to the Greeks.

2 What is the effect of Colley's finery?

3 What does Talbot mean by the Church and the State?

4 How much do we learn here about what happens to Colley?

5 What is the threat to 'social stability' mentioned by Talbot?

6 What is the meaning of Colley's exclamation 'Joy! Joy! Joy!'?

Chapter 51

Another passage of reflection. Talbot is bored and still looks on the Colley episode as entertainment (the word is his) sadly lacking since. But Talbot's lofty boredom does not save him from a misunderstanding with Deverel, to whom he proposes that Zenobia be bestowed on Colley, to save them both trouble. Deverel knows what Talbot does not: that Colley is homosexual. That is Deverel's 'jest' (page 121).

mixed metaphor One which confuses several terms, as in the previous sentence.
inamorata Beloved (Latin).
épris Taken (French).

Revision question on Chapter 51

1 What is a mixed metaphor?

Chapter ALPHA

Talbot records Colley's seclusion in his cabin without any sense of impending doom. He is more interested in the fact that Brocklebank's female companions are not relations but mistresses.

κωφὰ πρόσωπα Deaf mutes.

Revision questions on Chapter ALPHA

1 What is Talbot's attitude to Colley now?

Chapter 60

In this chapter Summers nervously confronts Talbot with his responsibility for Colley's predicament. To his credit, Talbot begins to acknowledge this and is ready to do something about it. On the other hand, a general sense of self-esteem prompts him almost as strongly, and the whole chapter is a subtle psychological study.

The text consists of two lengthy conversations between Summers and Talbot punctuated by Talbot's visit to Colley. In the first conversation, Summers reproaches Talbot with his patronizing manner and exploitation of his privileges, and persuades him that a visit from him will help Colley recover his self-esteem. The visit produces no effect, and Summers then tells Talbot that he is ultimately responsible for Colley's fate, because he angered the captain by his visit – an anger which could be vented only on Colley, not on Talbot himself. Thus, his privilege could be said to have caused the problem, and Summers believes it will help to solve it: Talbot must persuade the captain to visit Colley. Talbot agrees. In this chapter we see a stage in Talbot's development. He is still superior, detached, complacent; but it appears that these faults can also work to advantage by forcing him to confront what he would rather avoid.

60 Having neglected his journal, Talbot now begins again to keep it in detail.

Perfect translation The theme of translation or interpretation pervades the novel, here applied to class.

Newtonian Force Gravity.

misjudged your character Now it is Summers' turn to wrestle with the problem of interpreting.

laws of nature Summers accepts that the class system is inevitable – part of nature. But the novel implicitly questions that view.

what is time in a theatre? A significant question. In the ship, as in a theatre, the normal pressures and habits of daily life are suspended and others put in their place. Hence the heightening of the atmosphere.

Noblesse oblige Rank imposes obligations.

fair play Interestingly, Talbot substitutes a more generous notion for Summers' – suggesting a basic capacity for goodness in spite of his frivolity and snobbery. But he still patronizes Summers ('Fear nothing, man').

as bad as parsons A phrase which signals Talbot's contempt for clergymen at a crucial moment, just before he enters Colley's cabin.

handsome enough Note Talbot's complacency.
Classes Plantarum *The Classes of Plants* – a work on botany.
Saints Everlasting Rest By Richard Baxter (1615–1691) – exactly the sort of book such a clergyman would have.
a pile of manuscript This turns out to be Colley's letter.
stand shot Stand firm in the face of fire.
You Summers brings home Talbot's responsibility to him.
didactic Tutorial.
new and unformed society Australia, like America (established only thirty years before the action of the novel) is to be a country without the old institutions and prejudices.
least force The principle already enunciated by Talbot.
'Justice' This is the common theme of the Greek tragedians referred to earlier (page 104).

Revision questions on Chapter 60

1 What are the arguments Summers offers to provoke Talbot into action?

2 How does Talbot respond to these arguments, and what do his responses reveal about his character?

3 Explain the phrase *noblesse oblige* and its significance here.

Chapter 61

Talbot beards the captain on deck and reveals to Anderson that he keeps a detailed diary – thus communicating to him that he has a complete record of the fiasco involving Colley, and Anderson's part in letting it happen. Talbot returns to his cabin and shortly afterwards, as he predicted, observes Anderson come down to Colley's cabin. But the captain cannot persuade himself to go in and, after a moment's hesitation, turns round and goes back up to his own deck.

a regular stitcher A big row.
moghool Emperor – a corruption of the Persian word for Mongol.
The tyrant . . . possible The ironic allusion is to moral as well as physical decay.
Hibernia Ireland.
Circe In Homer's *Odyssey*, the sorceress who transformed the sailors into swine. The allusion is clearly ironic – but more so than Talbot himself understands.
Mr Gibbon The historian of the Roman empire (1737–1794). The story goes that the dim-witted Duke of Gloucester, being introduced to the

author of *Decline and Fall of the Roman Empire* – a lengthy volume – remarked 'Scribble, scribble, scribble, eh, Mr Gibbon?'
statist Statesman.

Revision questions on Chapter 61

1 What do the Captain's quarters tell us about him?

2 Describe Anderson's reactions to Talbot.

3 What is the significance of Talbot's journal?

4 What is a statist? Why does Talbot discuss it?

Chapter BETA

Captain Anderson sends down Summers to look in on Colley, who still remains silently on his bed amid the stench. Summers begs Talbot to make another effort with Colley. He agrees, but to no avail. Summers believes that Colley is willing himself to death. After Summers leaves, Talbot realizes that the pile of manuscript previously on Colley's table is now missing. He returns to Colley's cabin, finds the papers and removes them, assuming that they prove Colley's case against Anderson's appalling behaviour. The captain sends Wheeler to invite Talbot to dine.

In this chapter we observe Talbot making some progress in sympathetic identification with Colley's state of mind, in spite of the ludicrously inappropriate story he tells about his own college days (page 152). In retrospect, however, the most significant thing about the chapter is the conversation between Summers and Talbot about what did or did not happen. It seems that Summers knows more than Talbot, and is preparing to conceal it, but this is not certain, even later in the novel. Once again we encounter the problem of interpretation. How can we ever know the truth of what goes on in the hearts and minds of others?

sanded Used to blot the page before blotting paper came into use.
Minerva The Greek goddess of Wisdom.
'You know . . . himself?' Talbot does not know – but Summers does.
bosky Tipsy.
***cannot* despair** Despair is a sin, for it contradicts the certainty of salvation revealed in the Bible.
'All?' We sense here that Summers is trying to find out how much Talbot knows.

There had been a time . . . Talbot is beginning to enter imaginatively into Colley's state of mind.

Revision questions on Chapter BETA

1 Why would Talbot's reflections on the captain's motives be best kept to himself?

2 How much does Summers know about what Colley did?

3 A Christian cannot despair. Why not?

4 How does Colley react to Talbot's visit?

Chapter GAMMA

In this chapter the process of Talbot's enlightenment is continued by two things: dining with the captain and reading Colley's letter. Talbot reaches the captain's quarters to find that he is dining in the company of Summers and Oldmeadow. He has a long talk with the captain before they arrive. At dinner they discuss Colley, and Anderson insists on summoning Brocklebank, on the pretence that he has some medical knowledge. The painter arrives tipsy and soon becomes drunk, talking about his craft as a painter of naval scenes, when the dinner is interrupted by Summers, who left earlier, to report the death of Colley. The captain asks Summers, Talbot and Oldmeadow to inspect the body. Oldmeadow faints. Brocklebank, who has returned to his cabin, drunk, staggers out half-naked mumbling about a low fever – words the captain latches onto to provide a reason for death. At the end of the chapter the captain resolves to record the incident accordingly in his log; while Summers presses Talbot to record a different version of events – the true version – in his diary. But Talbot has already resolved to do this, and the chapter ends with his reading of Colley's letter and its insertion into his journal.

The chapter is a macabre mixture of farce and horror, ranging from Brocklebank's drunken stagger to the stench in the dead man's cabin. It is the longest single stretch of prose in the book and one of the most intriguing. Its function in the overall structure of the book is to lead up to the discovery of Colley's letter, and to preface that discovery with the clearest possible demonstration of the captain's moral evasiveness. Anderson, it appears, prefers plants to people, and this preference colours his attitude. The sea-gardener 'must accustom himself to loss' (page 161) Anderson tells Talbot, and this is the approach he intends to adopt to his problem with Colley. The chapter offers a detailed study of the captain's misanthropy, inviting us to set it beside Summers' humanitarian concern and Talbot's more guarded sense of something seriously wrong which must be righted in the name of Justice. It also reveals Anderson's resentment – the end of the war effectively means the end of his career – and here, too we need to compare his attitude with Summers' readiness to risk promotion albeit nervously, and Talbot's realization that his own position in life is not quite so secure as he had imagined. Colley's humiliation and death poses problems for all concerned.

climbing plants Thus is explained the plant cultivated by Willis.
Eve The allusion to Genesis suggests the image of Anderson as Adam – though it may also add a hint of sexual ambivalence.
Garland Plant Stephanotis.
ancients i.e. Ancient Greeks.
Sir Joseph Banks The eminent botanist and plantsman.
the weather The delicate comedy of this scene is contained in Talbot's question and Anderson's reply.
Family As we are to discover, Talbot has touched on a sore point.
romancier Novelist, storyteller.
the expelled Adam The allusion is a telling one in a story concerned with good and evil, innocence, guilt and justice.
the ship's log Anderson is doing to Talbot what Talbot did to him: making him understand that a written record of events exists – in Anderson's version.
'No heel taps' A heel tap is the thickness of liquor left at the bottom of a glass. The phrase means: Drink Up!
Lucullus Roman general (117–58 BC) noted for lavish living.
Aesculapius Greek god of medicine.
the death of Lord Nelson This occurred at the Battle of Trafalgar (1805).
Queer Street Serious financial trouble.
London Particular A very thick fog. Apparently deriving from the name of a favourite London drink – Madeira (which is thick and brown).
lithograph A print from stone.
Fuseli 18th-century artist (1741–1825) who did a series of scenes from Homer, from whose *Iliad* 'The Shield of Achilles' is a scene.
K! Knighthood.
Verisimilitude Close imitation of reality. Having elaborated images from writing and the theatre Golding now turns to painting for a further discussion of understanding and translation.
Your client will return This long monologue reflects directly on the attempts of both Talbot and Anderson to give a credible account of events

in their 'logs'. Like Anderson, Brocklebank makes adjustments to the literal truth.

the man is dead Golding chooses the moment of maximum tension to introduce this announcement.

most of the emigrants The last time they so gathered was on the occasion of Colley's downfall.

Silenus A satyr, the foster father of Bacchus, god of wine. Compare Brocklebank's unashamed behaviour with Colley's.

tarred object in chains i.e. the corpse of an executed man hanging on the gallows.

Cornish Oldmeadow refers to a local superstition against touching corpses.

What women Talbot still does not understand the nature of Colley's catastrophe.

commissions Sins of commission are bad deeds positively done. Sins of ommission involve neglecting to do what we should do.

Revision questions on Chapter GAMMA

1 Why does the captain invite Talbot to dinner?

2 What do we learn about Anderson from his plants?

3 Is there any symbolism in this chapter?

4 What is the effect of Brocklebank's interruption?

5 Why does the captain send for Brocklebank?

6 What relevance to the book does Brocklebank's long discourse on painting have?

7 Describe and account for Talbot's state of mind at the end of this chapter.

Colley's letter

The first pages of the letter to Colley's sister have been lost. Nor is there a description of his last humiliation – on the contrary, the manuscript ends on a note of hope and rejoicing as Colley is about to go out and bring the people to repentance, an exploit which goes very seriously wrong – but otherwise we are offered an alternative account of the voyage to compare with Talbot's; an account which includes things the other leaves out, and vice versa.

Colley is mainly concerned with three issues: the extraordinary change in climate and atmosphere as the boat proceeds southwards;

his encounters with various people aboard; and his own problematic status as a clergyman when he sees himself despised and rejected. The three issues are linked. As the climate changes Colley, like Talbot, finds his senses and his feelings disoriented – a process begun by the sea-sickness both experience at the beginning of the trip, and which confuses their normal distinctions between physical and emotional states. As this process advances it affects the relationships of the travellers, loosening the normal bonds of obligation and respect and opening the way for the violent events which result in Colley's death. Colley's encounters take several different forms: with the passengers in general, with Talbot, with the sailors he admires, with the sympathetic Summers and Phillips, and – most important of all – with the captain. Apart from Summers, none of them respect his clerical role, an experience he finds baffling and disturbing.

The central events described in the letter are Colley's three meetings with the captain; his immersion in the badger bag, which occurs between the second and third of those meetings; and his final preparations to go among the ship's company. At their first encounter the captain is outrageously rude; but it is on the second occasion, when Anderson knocks Colley down, that the potential violence of the situation becomes apparent. The Captain's assault gives the signal, as it were, for Deverel and Cumbershum to manhandle Colley into the awning filled with execrement – as Anderson tacitly admits on his third meeting with Colley, when he comes as close to an apology as he is capable of doing. But there is a sense in which the third meeting is the most ominous of all. Anderson does nothing to prevent Colley from his foolhardy venture among the sailors; and although he cannot possibly anticipate what is going to happen, it is his duty to supervise such an occasion, or at least to make sure that it is supervised. To that extent Anderson is directly responsible for Colley's fate.

so I have . . . The missing pages evidently detail sea-sickness and the unpleasant behaviour of fellow-passengers. Little does Colley know that 'the most trying of my experiences' is yet to come. His ignorance is later seen to be ironic.

nameless creatures A reference to the prostitutes who ply their trade on the waterfront. Again, this becomes ironic in retrospect.

Old Albion Britain.

priedieu Prayer-desk.

lives and has his being A reference to Acts of The Apostles, 17,28.

servant! Colley is not used to such a luxury.

an oceanic paradise! This contrasts sharply with Talbot's earlier and Colley's later images of hell.

Juno Queen of the Roman gods.
Manston Place Colley, like Talbot, has a patron.
SAVIOUR . . . *anchor* Colley, like Talbot, takes his comparisons from his surroundings – but Christianity already draws much of its imagery from the sea.
England's Hero! Nelson. Colley's romantic daydreams are a clue to his subsequent fate: there is, as Talbot notices, a theatrical streak in him.
manly forms The first of several allusions in the letter to the attractiveness of the sailors which hints at Colley's homosexual desires.
proper portion Buttocks. Colley, like Talbot, has a somewhat arch, pompous literary style which uses periphrasis, round-about expressions.
astonishing world Colley echoes Talbot's comparison of the ship to a world.
sidestays Beams supporting the sides.
halyards Ropes for hoisting sails.
awe Another hint foreshadowing Colley's fate at the sailors' hands.
Sophocles The tragedian alluded to by Talbot.
The sky . . . Like Talbot, Colley breaks out of his formal language into lyrical description.
The human mind . . . Also Talbot's sentiment. For Colley, too, the physical immensity and insecurity of the sea bring on moral and spiritual uncertainties.
intellect . . . *heart* The distinction between reason and feeling is important in the novel. Colley is ultimately led astray by feeling, but Talbot later wonders whether rational calculation would really have been preferable.
thunderbolt . . . Talbot omits this episode.
decency Ironic, in view of what happens to Colley.
HIS AWFULNESS The strangeness of the journey makes Talbot think of Man and Colley of God.
a separate world Colley here elaborates Talbot's image. The parallels between the two journals are significant, allowing us to compare the development of the two writers directly.
how deep . . . In context, the innocent question takes on a wider meaning. The portentousness of Smiles's reply points to the moral abyss in which Colley is to find himself. On a simpler level, we can see emerging in him the disturbing ideas and emotions which provide fertile ground for the subsequent catastrophe to grow in.
reprehensible superstition . . . Colley underestimates their capacity for superstition. Compare pages 56–60.
Republicans and Jacobins Colley refers to the French Revolution. The Jacobins were among the more extreme revolutionaries. But whereas Talbot objects to the Revolution on political grounds, Colley's dislike is religious. In his eyes Mr Prettiman is a free-thinker i.e. an atheist. The Revolution was – wrongly – associated with atheism.
wild halo . . . The comedy of Colley's doubts about Prettiman matches the comedy of Talbot's snobbery.
a Miss Brocklebank Compare Colley's response to Zenobia with Talbot's.

a young gentleman Colley singles out Talbot as Talbot singles out Colley – but on very different grounds. Nevertheless the symmetry is significant. They are drawn to one another – Colley by admiration, Talbot by distasteful curiosity.

such birth Like Summers, Colley accepts Talbot's natural superiority.

flashes of lightning Another storm unrecorded by Talbot. They prefigure Colley's own 'storm'.

the awfulness What had at first seemed a paradise begins to look like hell.

disordering of the intellects! This goes deeper than Colley knows (the plural is archaic).

Homer's 'Unfurrowed ocean.' Talbot, too, quotes Homer – but in Greek. Greek.

an opacity Colley's sense of the physical world is intensified by his sea-journey. He is aware of both its mystery and its threatening power. This awareness prefigures the human power which is to destroy him.

robust . . . century Colley refers to the rationalist philosophers whose ideas helped to shape the French Revolution, and of whom Prettiman is a faint echo; and the scientists whose work raised awkward questions to about Genesis.

They . . . ships! From Psalms, 107,23.

the moon . . . head! Colley and Talbot experience similar forms of physical and emotional disorientation.

the plain facts Colley's narrative is actually quite detailed, even bringing out the comedy in his humiliation.

sectarianism i.e. Methodism or Quakerism, the two main movements which split off the Church of England to become sects. Colley deplores them as much as Talbot does.

I am a clergyman Colley thinks at least as highly of his profession as Talbot does of his birth.

some support In his own way Colley is just as attached to the established order as Talbot is.

drunkenness An ironic anticipation of what is to come.

tears of shame Colley's ability to admit this to himself is important. If he were able to reinterpret his experience he might be better able to cope with it. Honesty helps to destroy him.

At sea . . . suffers Another ironic anticipation of his fate.

Mr Summers pointed . . . Summers tactfully gets the boy out of the way.

Repeat your lesson! There is indeed a kind of madness about the ferocity of the captain's behaviour. This is an abuse of the duly constituted power for which both Colley and Talbot have so much respect – an abuse which brings not only the captain's character but also the nature of that power into question.

had I not heard . . . Talbot Overhearing plays a role in the plot – as when Talbot hears Zenobia with a lover.

***true* gentleman** The question of what constitutes a gentleman is considered throughout the book. Born a gentleman, Talbot nevertheless has to learn a rather different notion of what it means.

***that* only I could do** Which is precisely what Colley does do.
my Master Jesus.
amended, altered, softened Talbot comes to the same conclusion.
THOSE FEET Colley's sense of abasement before Jesus painfully anticipates his sexual abasement before Billy Rogers.
Robinson Crusoe Solitary hero of the novel by Defoe (1660–1731) who refers to the island he is stranded on as his kingdom. The allusion underlines Colley's sense of isolation.
a true friend to religion Colley never learns how mistaken he is.
a young lady Colley is as mistaken about Zenobia as he is about Talbot.
Daring still . . . altar! This extraordinary passage, in which religious imagery and homoerotic feeling are equally mingled hints at Colley's complex motives for liking Talbot, in which social respect and sexual desire are linked. Now the letter is no longer directed to his sister he can express all his feelings, and reveal his naivety.
the hottest region The Equator – where rites of passage are traditionally performed, and where the climate easily disorders those from more temperate regions.
to spare me embarrassment Colley, like Talbot, mistakes – misreads – the motives of others.
'Civilization' After the episode in which he kisses the sleeping Talbot, this passage on the sailors reveals clearly the extent of Colley's homosexuality. The world of friendship and even love in which the men appear to live, is deeply attractive when contrasted with the highly ordered relationships among the passengers. The all-male life is romanticized, and we see that Colley also senses the sexual freedom the sailors have – a freedom which turns out to be catastrophic for him when it is revealed as a kind of anarchy by the episode of his downfall.
passes the love of women This Biblical phrase (2 Samuel, 1,26) has a double connotation. It refers in context to brotherly love between men, but has also acquired a homoerotic connotation. It is this which is to prove disastrous for Colley – another example, perhaps, of misreading.
strange sounds The sounds of Talbot's love-making with Zenobia.
enthusiasm! Ironically Colley suspects Talbot of the very failing Talbot suspects in him.
These attacks . . . devotion A rather different kind of too passionate devotion brings about Colley's downfall.
that ceremony Colley's reaction to this 'rite' underlines the ambivalence of his feelings for the sailors.
one young fellow Billy Rogers.
rum . . . ichor The Greek parallel is appropriate, hinting at the Grecian cult of the beautiful youth, to be found in the work of i.e. Plato.
Nemean Lion Lion slain by Hercules, in Greek Mythology.
I heard a furnace roar The furnace of Colley's own desire.
to kneel before him Precisely what Colley eventually does.
But he went . . . not go The description which follows these suggestive

words underlines the sailor's flirtatiousness, as he displays his body for all to see.

a living thing The sense of the sea as a great animal suggests danger, for the ship is in the power of the animal – just as Colley is drifting into the power of his daydreams and desires.

effluvias Disagreeable vapours, arising from the ship's waste. The pervasive image of foulness hints at moral decay and the threat of a general rottenness arising from the whole body of people aboard.

find no peace Colley mistakes Talbot's sexual restlessness for mental and spiritual stress.

a missive The love-letter Zenobia loses.

sartorial Clothing. Perhaps this does indeed suggest to Cumbershum and Deverel their later treatment of Colley. It takes up the theme of appearances and dress about which Colley is so concerned.

Sortes Virgilianae Divination (Latin). It was a medieval habit to open the Bible or Virgil's *Aeneid* at random and take the lines landed on as an oracle. The results were usually as comically indirect as Colley's.

strangeness The strangeness is to increase violently.

'paranomasia' Play upon words. Colley refers to the ship which carries him but which might also be used to 'transport' convicted felons. However, there is a further play on the word, suggesting that the ship brings him to ecstasy – which it does in a most unexpected way, so that, after the event which ultimately destroys him, Colley emerges with the word Joy on his lips.

sanctified . . . And therefore untouchable. Colley is sadly mistaken in this expectation.

spy through the knot Like Talbot, Colley is seeing the world in a new way – and therefore seeing himself in a new way. The description which follows shows him his appearance as though for the first time, as if stirred by his new sexual feelings to a sense of his own body.

a beggar Colley's sudden perception of his own absurd appearance looks forward to the grotesquerie of the carnival, when the sailors appropriate his academic dress, and he appears drunk and semi-naked.

language of navigation Like Talbot, Colley is absorbing a new vocabulary – which symbolizes the new life he is entering into.

between two paragraphs Colley echoes Talbot's narrative tricks.

the poor light . . . distance Colley is oblivious to the truth of the matter: he has literally become a scapegoat and therefore an outcast.

an awning This is the bath in which Colley is to be immersed.

till my dying day Colley speaks more truly than he knows.

red sun . . . full moon These words recall the Coleridge poem already cited several times in the novel, *The Ancient Mariner*.

very scales of GOD Words recalling the phrase 'scales of justice'. A few lines later, Cumbershum and Deverel announce that they have come to take Colley to judgment. The symbolism is unmistakeable: as in Shakespearian tragedy, nature appears to reflect the world of Man.

cathedra Chair.

Next day

***part* of my mind** Such is the atmosphere on the ship, intensified by the equatorial heat and humidity, that Colley has a sense of supernatural horror, though he knows he is being tormented by human agency.
demonic The imagery of hell, invoked by Talbot, is now fulfilled.
crowned with flame The presiding figure (Neptune, god of the sea) is also Satanic.
half-naked Colley appears thus in public for the second time, unwillingly. Stripped of his vestments he is completely vulnerable.
made to kneel The humiliation foreshadows his encounter with Billy Rogers.
I was the foe! This repeated phrase bears a good deal of weight. The ceremonies involved in Crossing the Line appear to descend from pagan rites of initiation – in which context a Christian clergyman would inevitably be 'the foe'. But Colley has also taken on the role of scapegoat. Like a wounded animal, his humiliation at the captain's hands has made him vulnerable to the ferocity of his fellows as a mob (a point confirmed by the references to the victims of the French Revolution). Colley takes upon himself the filthiness of the crowd.
betwixt . . . ground As though falling off a horse.
explosion This is Prettiman's gun fired by Summers.
the devils . . . the *people* The analogy is clear. If the sailors had seemed like gods, all the people aboard now seem like devils.
I believe . . . myself again During the rest of his short life, Colley does indeed become 'himself' with results he could not begin to anticipate. He discoverers in himself an animal nature not unrelated to the bestiality of the audience of his shame.
victim . . . Anderson The persistent links made between Anderson and God, hint that the benevolent God of Colley's theology is a myth, and that the true God, if there is one, may reflect the cruelty of the powerful Anderson. At the highest level, the novel is a reflection on the nature of evil and its sources: Man or God?
SAVIOUR'S Colley's discourse seems to open up a gap between the loving Saviour – identified with Talbot – and the fierce God, identified with Anderson. Billy Rogers plays an ambivalent role: apparently Saviour, but actually destroyer.
interior Colley's distinction between the exterior events of his shame, and the interior events of his interpretation of that shame reflect his confusion about the distinction between appearance and reality and his failure so far to understand the implications of his own feelings and desires.
Great Truths . . . Religion! The capital letters suggest a divergence between Colley's conviction and the facts of the case, by making it seem as though he is merely falling back on conventional, unexamined wisdom.
Square Mortar board.
'I know it, Mr Colley.' Anderson's admission shows that he knows full well what has been done, an important point when he later tries to cover up

'Are you mad?' Anderson warns Colley of the possible consequences. In a sense, this diminishes his responsibility for what follows.
his Master A comic misunderstanding which reveals the distance between Colley and the others.
All was now to be well A tragic irony.
WORD i.e. the word of God.
revoke Colley is sadly deluded.
the blue, the green . . . foam! Another allusion to *The Ancient Mariner*.

Revision questions on Colley's letter

1 What is the effect of Colley's reminiscences of youth?

2 Describe Colley's attitude to the ordinary sailors. How do they compare for him with the officers?

3 List the literary allusions in this section and comment briefly on the relevance of each one.

4 What is Colley's feeling about the ocean? Does it change?

5 What does religion mean to Colley?

6 In what ways does the letter use the description of physical objects to convey ideas or emotions?

7 How honest is Colley with himself about his own motives?

8 How does Colley explain Anderson's behaviour, and what does he think of it?

9 Describe Colley's feelings for (a) Talbot, (b) Rogers. Are they the same?

10 How does Colley respond to the badger bag episode?

11 What is Colley's state of mind at the end of his letter, and why?

12 List any uses of irony in this letter, conscious or otherwise.

13 What do his clothes mean to Colley?

14 Is Colley wise or reckless to venture among the sailors?

Colley's letter ends on a note of optimism with preparations for his visit to the lower orders. The morning after Talbot reads the manuscript, he is roused by Wheeler with the news that there is to be an enquiry, conducted by Summers, Talbot and the Captain.

Witnesses explain how Colley agreed to drink rum in a spirit of reconciliation, and how the sailors took him down below. Billy Rogers, who took Colley back to his quarters, insists that Colley was drunk. When Anderson, who has been primed with information by his spy, Wheeler, challenges Rogers to admit to indecently assaulting Colley, Rogers threatens to expose the officers on board who have been involved in homosexual activities. He is dismissed, and the captain insists on concluding the enquiry. Talbot refuses to sign the captain's report on Colley's death, offering a signed statement of his own instead. Colley is buried at sea.

Anderson's demand that Talbot record in his journal that this is a happy ship (page 258) is rendered grimly farcical by the events of this chapter, which reveal a yawning chasm of deceit and suspicion, surrounding the sinister figure of Billy Rogers, the handsome sailor with whom Colley disgraced himself. Talbot, like Colley, recognizes Rogers's sexual magnetism though from a detached point of view: he notes the animal beauty of the man's body. Rogers's skilful evasion of the truth, together with Wheeler's spying and the Captain's own manoeuvering to avoid responsibility for what has happened, constitute a web of intrigue issuing from the hidden life of the ship – in part, the life of the sailors, who most of the passengers (except Colley) take for granted. It seems that Colley's vision of naval fraternity was wide of the mark: on the contrary, each man is locked in his own vice or solitude.

rousted . . . end-for-end Hauled in.
informant Wheeler, who acts as the captain's spy.
criminal assault The captain insists on raising the matter in the expectation that it will get him off the hook.
wide-eyed candour Deceitful appearances. Colley, who looked so ugly, had a fine spirit lacking in the magnificent Rogers.
go about Change direction.
enemies! Compare Colley's discovery that he is the foe. Now it is Rogers's turn to be like a cornered animal.
we This harks back to Colley's remark 'What a man does defiles him . . .' (page 235)
'Shall I . . . sir?' Rogers neatly turns his problem back on the captain.
Can your . . . to that? A remark which bears out Anderson's claim that mud would stick, however innocent the accused.
a *happy* ship Anderson has a grimly ironic sense of humour.
flintlocks Guns.
unblooded Bare.
ceremony strange This is another 'rite of passage'.

cruxes Puzzling passages.
Aeneid Narrative poem by the Roman poet Virgil.
bullion Gold braid.
sky pilot Clergyman. (In fact this term did not come into use until after the period in which the novel is set.)
clewed up Tied up to the yards.
hove to Stationary.
Davey Jones Familiar sea-term for the devil. It seems that Colley is literally going to the devil.
sternpost Timber supporting the rudder.
pintles Bolts.
started . . . summons The quotation is from Talbot's favourite playwright, Shakespeare: *Hamlet*.
envoi Farewell.
Richard . . . again Another quotation from Shakespeare: *Richard II*.
in keeping . . . i.e. Because they are involved with death.
deeper . . . sound Shakespeare again. This time *The Tempest*.
have recourse to Shakespeare! Characteristically Talbot thinks of literature to do his feeling for him.
stun's'ls Narrow sails set at the edges of large square sails when the wind is light.
traverse board A circular board marked like a compass and used to determine the ship's cargo from watch to watch i.e. every half hour.

Revision questions

1 How does the captain conduct the enquiry?

2 Describe Rogers's attitude throughout his questioning.

3 Why is Rogers dismissed?

4 Why does Talbot refuse to sign the enquiry findings?

5 Identify the Shakespearian quotations in this chapter. What is the point of them?

Chapter &

Wheeler has disappeared, apparently fallen overboard. Deverel, stinging with the captain's rebuke for his part in Colley's mistreatment, tells Talbot Anderson's history. The Captain hates clergymen because he is the illegitimate son of a great lord who married his mistress off to a clergyman. This also accounts for Anderson's ambivalent feelings towards his social superiors.

Mr Prettiman has become engaged to Miss Granham, who is

organizing a play to amuse the passengers. During a conversation Mr Prettiman reveals – without realizing what he said – that the act which shamed Colley to death was not buggery but fellatio; he was not assaulted but took part willingly.

In the last chapter Talbot returns to an earlier playful style, fancying the action he has just described as though it were a play and making witty conversation with fellow passengers. Yet the style is now, like the man, a little chastened, and a little richer thereby. The comedy is no longer callow or complacent; the cynicism is darker and more perplexed. At the end of the book Talbot remains the man he was – worldly, lofty, affable – but in a different key.

ampersand The sign representing 'and'.
Colley's drama This phrase raises a number of issues concerning Talbot's whole approach to life: his tendency to remain detached, to turn moral questions into aesthetic ones, to retreat into a worldly style when faced with difficult or profound problems. On the other hand, the chapter shows him wrestling with just these problems, and facing the uncertainty of this drama's conclusion.
all, all alone Another quotation from *The Ancient Mariner.*
bathos Anticlimax. The pun depends on Colley's immersion in the sea.
Thalassian Oceanic.
real life . . . given book This is a perplexing passage. We understand the literal sense. On the other hand, *Rites of Passage*, the novel, is devoted to Colley's drama, its length determined accordingly. In the last chapter Golding pulls together some of the literary jokes he has been teasing us with throughout, concerning the relationship between art and life, appearance and reality, truth and fiction. The novel, after all, is comic, though the subject is tragic. So how are we supposed to take it? That question remains unanswered.
He *was* being sought The action of the story catches up with Talbot's narrative, interrupting it.
deaths . . . slippers . . . Observe the grotesque juxtaposition of the serious and the trivial, a feature of this novel – and another example of bathos.
Literature . . . on it! A reiteration of the earlier point. But Summers replies that life does have a form, determined by birth and death.
'Roustabout' A tiny detail of wordplay of the sort Golding likes. The confusion springs from Tommy Taylor's words at the bottom of page 248.
mooing Talbot's disdain surfacing again.
blank pages Another literary joke: for in writing about their blankness, Talbot is helping to fill them.
limping after the drama Talbot returns again to the point about the form of art and the formlessness of life.
satyr . . . trilogy The ancient Greek playwrights of whom Talbot spoke much earlier in the novel were accustomed to write short tragedies in

groups of three, to be performed one after another, and followed by a comedy or satyr play.

dénouement Unravelling of the plot.

laws of the service Navy regulations. An officer may not challenge his superior to a duel.

marches with Shares a border with.

keeping i.e. as a mistress.

Wesleyan Charles Wesley (1707–1788) was the founder of Methodism – hence the ironic tone.

barker! Shot.

good Edmund Yet another allusion to Shakespeare, this time to *King Lear*. The allusion is complicated in context by the fact that, in the play, Edgar is dispossessed by his wicked half-brother Edmund. It is complicated even further by the fact that, as the scion of an impoverished family, Deverel no doubt feels the jealousy of Talbot, Edmund felt of Edgar and Anderson of his half-brother.

all to seek Completely out of order.

a lord's gallantry Talbot clearly forgets he is writing for his godfather, who is almost certainly just such a lord (see the penultimate paragraph on page 55).

Deverel's *jest* Here is a case of Talbot's art imitating Anderson's life.

a *play!* They turn to acting a play when reality no longer offers enough amusement – a grim comment on their treatment of Colley, as Talbot's talk of a drama on page 264 tacitly acknowledges.

Shaman Wizard.

our own clergy Miss Granham trumps Talbot, who believes he holds similarly 'enlightened' views about the clergy. It shows how little he has thought out the implications of his views – and how it would be if everyone shared them.

fiançailles Engagement (French).

Hymen God of marriage.

a great shame This shows up the stunning insensitivity of Deverel.

de mortuis Latin, short for *De Mortuis nil nisi bonum*: speak only good of the dead.

another form Talbot thinks Miss Granham knows about Colley's encounter (though he himself still thinks it was buggery).

true liberty The absurdity of the misunderstanding which follows – Mr Prettiman and Miss Granham think Colley was guilty of chewing tobacco – is underlined by the pomposity of the Granham/Prettiman conversation, which conjures up a comic picture of their wooing.

a roar of laughter A good example of bathos.

whoops It is not clear how many of the audience know or guess what happened, and how much they guess or know. But Summers has certainly understood the full truth, and perhaps others have sensed it. The comedy is therefore ambiguous: partly at Prettiman, partly because of Colley himself.

a change in . . . feelings It seems that laughter and the public airing of suspicions without anything being said, help the passengers to regain their equanimity.

dismissed Shakespeare Golding may be having a dig at some contemporary critics here. Talbot's reply reveals his own obtuseness as well as Prettiman's. Prettiman is indifferent to personal qualities and their significance in life; but Talbot should have learnt from his recent experiences that society consists of more than individuals. It is also composed of institutions which generate pressures of their own, as Colley found to his cost. The passing exchange reveals how much and how little Talbot has learnt.

Goethe (1749–1832) German poet and playwright.

the genius of one language This returns to the persistent theme of translation.

Gothic Savage. They are, of course, talking about Talbot.

links The pieces of evidence.

never a tempest Another reference to Shakespeare – and perhaps a hint that the story, unlike that of *The Tempest*, does not end happily.

Lo! . . . creep! Presumably Golding's own invention.

deboshed Debauched.

the sun and moon The final words of the book echo Colley's vision of the scales of Justice (page 233).

Revision questions on Chapter &

1 What is Talbot saying about the relationship between reality and fiction at the beginning of this chapter? What relevance does it have for the novel?

2 Why does Wheeler disappear?

3 Does Deverel's account of Anderson change our view of the captain's behaviour?

4 Explain the honour code by which Deverel acts.

5 Why do the others laugh at Prettiman's imitation of the sailor?

6 Why does Summers go along with the tobacco chewing theory?

7 'Man can die of shame.' Is this what the book is about?

Golding's art in *Rites of Passage*
The characters

The characters can be divided into three groups: the protagonists (Colley, Talbot and Anderson): the passengers (Brocklebank, Prettiman, Granham, and Zenobia): and the sailors (Summers, Cumbershum, Deverel, Rogers and Wheeler). Obviously, the three groups are not distinct: Anderson is a sailor, while Colley and Talbot are passengers. But the grouping is appropriate to their roles in the plot, which might be said to have Colley at its centre, with Anderson and Talbot pulling in different directions on either side, and the others disposed round about to play subsidiary roles. The central power struggle between Anderson and Talbot over the interpretation of Colley's death dictates what we know of the other characters (except Colley) whose roles are determined accordingly. The characters and their roles are absolutely central to the book, shaping the development of the plot, rather than vice versa, and highlighted against the crowd scenes which play an important part in the drama.

Colley

In one sense Colley is the novel's main character; in another he is merely the occasion for the action and the reflections it generates, recorded in his letter and in Talbot's journal. Colley is not merely a character: he is very much the embodiment of certain social and temperamental traits. Of comparatively humble birth, he has nevertheless been educated at university and taken holy orders. Like many before and since, he is going to Australia partly with a sense of mission, and partly because there is a better chance of preferment there for someone with no connections – a necessity in an age when family meant more than ability. This mixture of motives – revealed by his occasional reflection on the advantages of knowing Talbot – is not hypocritical. The structures of the society and the church to which Colley belongs recognized the necessity of a man making his way in the world and saw no contradiction between priestly vows and a modicum of worldly ambition. The Anglican church is founded on such common-sensical views. But, unfortunately for him, Colley does not have the comfortable character which would make this the path to a pleasant and useful life. He is an emotional, unstable, even passionate man, who has not yet learnt the art of compromise, despite injunctions to his sister to be nice to their patrons, and a lively sense of the value of good birth and nobility. He is also shy, awkward and ugly; naive and painfully self-conscious. This is a difficult combination at the best of times. In a confined space dominated by a captain who loathes clergymen, and has transmitted that loathing to a crew already disposed, by virtue of their occupation, to contempt, it is potentially disastrous. It needs only the releasing of Colley's homosexual longings to complete the catastrophe.

Colley is placed in a miniature society which reflects its parent, the England of the early nineteenth century, accurately but also intensely. The ship's confinement and the prospect of a long voyage – months rather than weeks – magnifies common attitudes and emotions, which can easily get out of hand unless kept under strict control – a point Summers understands well enough when he cautions Colley to beware of taking his zeal too far. In particular, attitudes on the ship echo the always ambivalent situation of clergymen, at once respected, feared and despised. The clergyman represents authority – the ultimate authority of salvation and damnation; but in an increasingly secular society, where the church is merely an arm of the state (as Talbot recognizes) rather than its dominant institution, such authority is precarious. For many it represents a tiresome obstacle to their freedom to fulfill desires – all the more tiresome because of a residual grudging sense that the obstacle is justified, that the moral and spiritual values the church stands for, however restrictive, are nevertheless right. This was the situation in early nineteenth-century England, and it is the situation Colley finds himself in aboard ship. The Church of England had fallen into particular contempt in the eighteenth-century when people perceived that its pretensions were all too often a mask for laziness and indifference; for prosperous parsons, endowed by the church and usually chosen from the upper and middle classes, to prefer their pleasures to their duties. This institutional decay was one reason for the rise of Methodism, which took prayer out of the church and into the fields and brought a new fire to religious observance, crossing class boundaries and emphasizing the ultimate authority not of the state or the church but of the individual soul. Anglicanism retained nominal respect as the official religion, but little more.

Colley is the heir to this state of affairs, which is reinforced aboard ship by the traditional indifference to religion of the tough ordinary seamen in particular, and the navy in general. As the representative of established religion he is thus vulnerable on all fronts: as a figure of moral authority, as a priest, as an establishment figure, and as a Christian who is bound to disapprove of the 'pagan' lusts and desires of his fellow men. This last point becomes particularly – and literally – important as the ship approaches the Equator. Not only do passions rise under the influence of boredom, the changing climate and the close proximity of the passengers; but the time for the Saturnalia of Crossing the Line approaches – the rites of passage of the novel's title. These ceremonies, usually harmless enough, nevertheless have a distant connection with occasions familiar in all societies, when normal social discipline is briefly suspended and the people participate in riotous behaviour – when 'anything goes'. Usually this freedom is no more than nominal: a village fête or carnival can be regarded as a tame kind of Saturnalia. Sometimes the significance is more profound and violent energies are released which cannot easily be controlled, except by the act of release – which is thought by many to be the original purpose of such Saturnalia. Such ceremonies also combine with the persecution of ritual victims, who take upon themselves the sins of their fellows and are ritually cast out. Once again, this is usually a matter of performance: the victim is not really banished or killed, but mimes the action. In some cases, however, the sacrifice is real. As a Christian, Colley cannot but be aware that such a sacrifice is at the very heart of his religion. Jesus was cast out, was destroyed, was made to carry the sins of the world and made an example of in a series of Saturnalian rituals – the casting of lots, the crown of thorns etc. – and a public execution along with common criminals. Thus Colley's predicament, as a contemptible clergyman approaching the Equator in a ship filled with violent and hostile men, brings together the traditions of pagan Saturnalia and sacrifice, and of Christian example on the one hand; with social contempt for the institution he represents on the other. These combine with his own weaknesses of character to bring about his catastrophe.

This lengthy comment on the historical context is necessary if we are to understand the violence of the action, which is presented for much of the time as a comedy. Golding has always been intrigued by symbolism – by the way in which certain things, persons and actions carry a greater weight than at first appears. Such is the case with Colley. His very insignificance, his absurdity, the contrast between his lofty ideals, the magnificent vestments which embody them, and the small ugliness of the man inside those vestments help to focus his symbolic value, as someone who is at the same time a victim and a protagonist. For as the many allusions in the text suggest, there is yet another historical model we must take into account when we try to make sense of Colley's fate: the model of Greek tragedy.

The Greek tragedians – especially Aeschylus and Sophocles – are preoccupied with the ironic contrast between the littleness of men, the grandeur of their pretensions, and the inexorability of fate.

Their protagonists are men who are driven to act as they do, and to bear the consequences of their actions, but who cannot avoid that action and those consequences. They are free to choose, but the choices are already circumscribed. They are weaker and more ignorant than they know, yet there is a magnificence in the resolution with which they meet their fate.

We can see evidence of such a predicament in Colley. There is, as he acknowledges when surveying himself in the mirror, no trace of the hero in Colley. He is nervous, fearful, vulnerable. Yet once on his path, he refuses to turn back, and at this stage he reveals that he, like his more heroic Greek models, is in the grip of hubris, the Greek word for pride. The difference lies in Colley's claim that this pride is dictated by loyalty to his Master i.e. Jesus, rather than by any personal motives. Yet his behaviour partially contradicts this – and his discovery of this contradiction helps to kill him as much as the shame of his sexual act. For as Colley remarks, it is what a man does that shames him, not what others do to him. What Colley has done is to yield to his own desire for Billy Rogers in the very act of carrying the word of God to the heathen sailors below decks, and to disgrace his calling at the very moment when he thought to have brought it most dignity. Like the heroes of Greek tragedies, though in unimaginably different circumstances, Colley has not known himself. He has overrated his own power and underrated the power of circumstances. What he took for trust in God turns out to be inextricably mixed with pride and lust.

Yet though Colley is the most unheroic of heroes – physically uncoordinated, knobbly-kneed, perpetually humiliated in public, at once farcical and pathetic – there is something fine about his determined insistence on confronting Anderson, about his refusal to compromise; and, above all, about his response to the meeting with Rogers, when he proclaims his joy (page 117). This occurs immediately after Talbot's description of his semi-naked body as a most unattractive sight, especially when we compare it with what we are told of the magnificent Rogers; and it is perhaps the most perplexing moment in the book. What are we to make of it?

The answer, I think lies in the fact that it is a revelation of Colley's deepest nature, a nature which is in violent conflict with his acquired role as a clergyman. Central to the novel are questions about the relationship between the natural and the conventional, the social and the personal, the general and the individual. Are we essentially ourselves, or are we what society makes us? It seems from Talbot's example, that each man likes to think of himself as a natural individual, and of others as conventionally constructed by society. I am simply myself, this view says, but you are the product of forces beyond your control. As Talbot discovers, the truth lies somewhere in between: we are all shaped by unknown forces, yet we all experience ourselves as individuals with an essential core, whether rightly or wrongly. But when the 'external forces' become too strong, we all feel our essential selves threatened: Anderson retreats to his garden, Talbot to his pose of lofty superiority, Colley into his clerical vestments. Paradoxically, we often feel more secure when we take up a role which seems to determine our sense of selfhood: captain, clergyman, man of the world. But 'external forces' operate at two levels: socially and biologically. Our sexual nature partakes of the self's paradox, for it is at once apparently part of our deepest individual nature, yet also an impersonal force which we cannot resist, and which equally often seems to be in opposition to our sense of identity, especially when that sexuality is in any way abnormal. This is the case with Colley. In his social being at once the very embodiment of conventional respectability and yet the object of contempt(for the reasons suggested above), in his biological being he is at once highly repressed (both because of his personality and his role as a clergymen) and yet, in the context, shockingly and violently abnormal, not only homosexual but passively so. He is thus in every respect torn by contradictions: a powerless figure of power, an erotic enemy of sensuous fulfillment, an ugly worshipper of beauty, a figure of authority who releases and is destroyed by anarchic forces. The joy which he experiences, albeit when drunk, after his act of love with Rogers, is joy indeed, for it is the one moment in his life when Colley's being, desires and actions – his whole self and the world it inhabits – are at one. The introvert is briefly an extrovert, the puritan a hedonist, the man of spirit a man of flesh. And as if to underline the point, he is literally nearly naked, uninhibitedly urinating on deck in front of the passengers, like a child or a savage – for one moment in life without the sense of shame which returns with redoubled force to destroy him.

Talbot

Talbot's aristocratic name immediately tells us a good deal about him. He is a familiar character in eighteenth-century and nineteenth-century English novels: the younger son or poor relation of a great family who has enough promise to interest the head of the family in his favour. Talbot is going out to Australia on employment with his patron's brother, who is some kind of governor. He has also been charged with a delicate mission by government agents, his task being to observe and report on the dissident freethinker and potential trouble-maker, Mr Prettiman. This suggests that he is already well thought-of in official circles as a dependable, discreet and loyal servant who will probably go far. However, in order to succeed he has to go far literally: the number of good posts at home is restricted, but for the 19th-century Englishman with the right connections, opportunities in the colonies were almost limitless, and Talbot looks forward to working in Australia for a few years, in order to earn his reward at home, where he has every intention of returning as soon as possible.

Golding is careful to build up Talbot's background and role in some detail for two reasons: so that we have enough information to interpret his narrative, and as a foil to Colley. The two men are sharply contrasted in character, attitude and destiny. Where Colley is awkward, emotional, absurd, at once repressed and wildly out of control, Talbot is the picture of elegant urbanity, and he knows it. Though we are not told that he is handsome, we can presume him to be good-looking in comparison with the bony Colley, though not sexually magnetic, like Rogers. But the difference between Talbot, Colley and Rogers, even in looks, is determined largely by class. Where Rogers has the earthy, primitive sensuality of the unregenerate proletariat which Talbot recognizes as close to the savage, Talbot himself sublimates his sexuality into personal authority over others, exercised through charm – a quality quite lacking in both Colley and Rogers. Charm is central to Talbot's character; it has become second nature, the very antithesis of Colley's gauche intensity. Talbot prides himself on turning off every situation, however awkward, with a smile, an elegant compliment, a witty remark. In fact, he puts his foot in it on several occasions – with Miss Granham, with Summers, with the Captain – revealing a gaucheness of his own: but it is typical that even this is forgiven him, and turned to account. His apologies only reinforce other people's sense of obligation to him for being so frank – a point he candidly acknowledges.

Yet although Talbot and Colley are sharply contrasted in manner, appearance, point of view, background and destiny, there are certain crucial points of comparison or even resemblance between them. This is suggested by the way in which their destinies, while not quite converging, do run close and parallel for a brief time. We are aware of a link between them early on in the book, when Talbot takes particular note of the parson, hovering between sympathy and contempt for this ludicrous figure. Talbot exemplifies a more general ambivalence in his attitude towards the clergy, whom he supports as pillars of established society, with which Talbot identifies himself, but despises for the very values they are supposed to espouse: love, charity, forgiveness, meekness. These values conflict with the code by which men such as Talbot and his patron live, a code designed for 'gentlemen' and based on honour, which is ultimately a form of pride. A gentleman is always able to act out of consideration for those weaker than himself because he rests secure in the sense of his own superiority – expressed, in a case such as Talbot's, through his amused detachment from the herd about him. Gentlemen exist on a plane of equality with one another, and their claims to this equality rest broadly on birth and education. A clergyman may be a gentleman up to a point, but his clerical role ultimately conflicts with the honour code. For one thing his holy orders debar him from defending his honour as effectively as the navy regulations prevent Deverel from 'calling out' Captain Anderson – and what is honour if it cannot be defended?

Without in any sense abandoning his way of life, Talbot is gradually brought to see that honour is not what he thought it. Colley's downfall at the hands of honourable men – Deverel and Anderson – suggests that the gentlemanly code is only a corruption of the values it is descended from, and that perhaps the degraded Colley had a closer link with those values than Talbot himself. For Talbot is not merely a typical example of his class: if he were that he would share the initial revulsion against Colley and the posthumous wave of sympathy for him in the lukewarm manner of the other passengers. The point about him is that he does begin to glean the inadequacy of his own attitude to life, and to see that a cynical detachment which involves doing one's duty in an adequate but perfunctory way may be enough in the common course of things, but not at such a moment of crisis.

Talbot, like Colley, is therefore a contradictory figure, and this is made apparent in a number of ways, above all in his combination of authoritarianism with a belief in justice and a taste for anarchic freedom for himself, if not for others. To begin with he sees the world as a place in which the rewards are rightly given to those clever enough to take them, including himself among this number; and he also sees such men as above the restrictions of common life to some extent. These restrictions – the moral code enforced by the church, for example – are necessary for the preservation of social order; but so long as superior beings observe the letter, there is no reason why they should not violate the spirit. It is fine for Talbot to have assignations with Zenobia, but these had better be discreet for two reasons, both selfish: so that Talbot is not associated with her in the public eye and can therefore retain complete freedom of action; and so they do not set a bad example to the lower orders. His plan for palming Zenobia off on Colley when he has done with her is, as he shamefacedly discovers when Deverel reveals the truth about Anderson, a ploy to allow him the enjoyment of power and pleasure without responsibility. It is about responsibility that he begins to learn a lesson from Colley – not in the commonsense meaning of simply accepting the consequences of our actions, but in a more metaphysical manner; for Colley has taken upon himself, albeit involuntarily, responsibility for the evil of his fellow passengers by being their victim and by acting out his deepest desires in a public scene. This is not a course Talbot could ever contemplate, but it does drive him to reflect on his own moral views, and to vow that he will not let the matter of Colley pass, but see that 'responsibility' for it lies where it should – with the captain and, as Summers says, with himself.

This recognition of moral equality does not, of course, entail an equal recognition of social equality. Like Colley, Talbot believes in the importance of social distinctions as essential to the fabric of society, though he is more cynical than Colley about their ultimate worth. It is Talbot, however, in his role as narrator, who focuses our attention on the comparison between the ship and the world, and points up the hierarchies, naval, worldly and heavenly, which interweave in the story. If Anderson is both captain and God, Colley both victim and sinner, what does that make Talbot? The answer is that, to begin with, Talbot sees himself as altogether outside any hierarchy that the church or the ship can offer. As a privileged traveller he is neither of the passengers nor of the crew. As an agnostic he sees the church only as a useful instrument. As for the world, he intends to rise above the state where hierarchies matter, and his social position has already given him a massive advantage in this respect – an advantage he shows no sign of abandoning. This superior quality is matched by his narrator's role, for the story-teller is always the one who knows more, who reveals the truth to the rest of us, like a god above his creations. Yet Talbot discovers that his role is not what it seems, that he has not known everything, or even very much. This is revealed, first when he discovers Colley's letter and then, after Colley's death, as he gradually pieces the mystery together. But that is what it remains: a mystery, something Talbot, for all his sophistication, cannot patronize, something permanently disturbing. That is the sense of his last words in the book.

Anderson

While it is left to Talbot to tell the story and to Colley to provide its substance, Anderson is the lynchpin of the action, for without his irrational hatred of clergymen it would not take place. His assault on Colley, in which he vents both his dislike and his resentment at having to grovel before Talbot, provides an example for the ship's company, who know they can treat the parson with impunity. Anderson's character is therefore vital to the novel.

It is one of Golding's complicated literary jokes that Anderson is made to be the illegitimate son of a nobleman, just as he might be in a cheap melodrama, and that this provides the apparently trivial motivation for Colley's tragic downfall – complicated because Talbot realizes that his plan for Zenobia to marry Colley echoes the fate of Anderson's mother. Literary convention and plot thus interweave in a very characteristic manner to unsettle our sense of the distinctions, between comic and tragic, serious and melodramatic, conventional and natural. Anderson is thus in the same relation to the English class system as both Colley and Talbot: a marginal figure who is *of* it but not really *in* it, his birth putting him in a limbo between the aristocracy and disgrace. Like Talbot and Colley, he is dependent on aristocratic patronage, but for him that patronage represents rejection, exclusion from his birthright. Now that the war, on which he depended for promotion, is coming to a close, Anderson knows that the same can be said of his career. There is nothing left for him but obscure retirement. This prospect exacerbates his natural misanthropy. He is determined to have solitude with his plants and to be absolute master in his own ship, while he has one, however inferior she may be – and her undoubted inferiority is another thorn in his side. His attack on Colley can therefore be seen not only as the product of his family circumstances, but as part of a pattern. Just as

Colley is heir to a discredited religious establishment, so Anderson is in part the victim of political circumstances: English inheritance laws and the end of the Napoleonic Wars. For all Colley's isolation, Talbot's superiority, Anderson's solitude, they are all three inescapably parts of a hugely complex social and historical fabric, which determines their range of possible choices.

Talbot and Colley both make comparisons, explicit and implicit, between the Almighty and Anderson, who is said to have god-like powers aboard ship. This is only partly a joke, for the captain does indeed have powers of life and death, though he is ultimately accountable for what he does to a higher authority. This accountability, however, is limited by the captain's ability to manage not only his ship but what is said about it. This we see Anderson doing in the account recorded in his log, and in the way he tries to manoeuvre Summers and Talbot into accepting his version of Colley's death. With Rogers, too, the captain is adroit enough to see that silence will be profitable for all concerned, whatever the truth of the matter. Summers understands that very well; but Talbot, a civilian beyond Anderson's authority, has other ideas. He wishes to see justice done, both for its own sake, but also because he resents the truly godlike power Anderson possesses: his completely arbitrary rule. The analogy here is not with the benevolent God of the New Testament, but with a savage deity who hands out rewards and punishments in ways which cannot be understood. When Deverel explains to Talbot the source of Anderson's bitterness, Talbot begins to understand the Captain's behaviour, but in the end it remains a mystery why he should take his violence to such lengths – just as it remains a mystery why Colley went so far, and why Talbot allows himself to become involved with Zenobia when he feels such distaste for her. Each man is driven by powers beyond his control, and in Anderson's case these powers have serious repercussions because of his extensive authority. It is one thing for Colley to go temporarily mad; it is quite another thing for Anderson.

The Captain's 'divine' powers are shown in an unexpected light when Talbot visits his quarters, where he finds Anderson watering his plants, and their conversation makes the comparison with the Garden of Eden explicit. But while he takes a delight in raising difficult plants, Anderson admits that sometimes they die: that is not within his control, especially when he has to sacrifice their water to his crew. This last admission reveals just how much he prefers plants to men. Yet at the beginning of the novel Talbot's attitude has not been so very different. Less contemptuous, he has nevertheless regarded others as the occasion for his amused contemplation, rather than as ends in themselves. Talbot learns to change this attitude, as the Captain does not. His last appearance in the book – at Colley's funeral – reveals him as just as misanthropic as ever. The terror of his crew, he is also their butt, as the nickname Rumbleguts suggests. He is feared but not loved, a savage deity indeed.

Miss Granham and Miss Brocklebank

There are only two significant female characters, a comically contrasted pair, whose differences we are invited to observe at their first introduction when Talbot meets his fellow passengers in Chapter X. By virtue of her parentage – daughter of an Anglican canon – Miss Granham counts as a lady. This is clearly of the highest importance to her. A former governess, she has striven to preserve her social rank, especially in the hurly-burly of the boat where all sorts of people are thrown together – hence her embarrassment when Talbot inadvertently forces her to reveal her profession. The point here is that 'ladies' do not work; but governesses have a strangely indeterminate status in this complex world of social distinctions because, although they are paid for their labour, it is not manual labour. They are therefore not classed with servants. As a result, the position of governess is a thoroughly unpleasant one, suspended in a kind of limbo between the drawing room and the servants hall, belonging to neither. Like so many of the other characters in this novel, Miss Granham is therefore marginal – someone from the edges of the society she is leaving. Her first response to this marginality is to maintain a fiercely ladylike stance: formal in speech, severe in manner, austere in morals. Ironically, she shares these traits with Mr Prettiman, and they are drawn together into a most unlikely union, considering his anti-religious views. But Miss Granham is able to transfer her puritanism quite easily from education to politics, from religion to reform, with such effect that, towards the end of the novel, Talbot – who has been briefed to watch Prettiman – resolves to keep a rather closer eye on the woman who is to become his wife.

No two women could be less alike than Miss Granham and Miss Brocklebank, the comically named Zenobia. The theatricality the name rightly suggests is a world away from Miss Granham's severe common sense. Miss Brocklebank's entire life is one long act, and this, too, is evident on her first appearance, when she speaks in an absurdly affected accent and behaves in an unsuitably girlish manner. The comic encounter between the two women (page 54) sums up their differences.

It eventually becomes clear that Zenobia is little better than a prostitute – hardly surprising, considering the character of her so-called father, Mr Brocklebank, in an age when the terms 'prostitute', 'actress', and 'artist's model' were more or less synonymous. Both Zenobia and the woman travelling as Mrs Brocklebank have been the painter's mistresses – a fact comically revealed when it turns out that the 'mother' is younger than the daughter. Zenobia's profession has more than comic interest, however: it plays a role in the unfolding of the plot and in the thematic development of the book. For it is his assignation with her which critically prevents Talbot from being present at Colley's immersion in the badger bag, and so, by delaying his realization of what is happening to the clergyman, postpones his offer of friendship to the man – an offer which might have been instrumental in avoiding the final catastrophe. Zenobia is also involved in the immediate causes of Colley's humiliation, by virtue of the note she receives from Billy Rogers, for it is Colley's interruption of the argument over that note between Deverel and Cumbershum which prompts them to victimize him.

Thematically, Zenobia is a focus of the sexuality which proves so explosive and so disastrous in the novel. Not only does she induce a feverish desire in Talbot, despite his clear realization that she is no more than a painted slut; she is also linked with Colley by their mutual 'relationship' with Billy Rogers, another focus of dangerous sexuality. Zenobia, as it were, represents the potency of appearances even when they are recognized as only that. To Colley she seems a beautiful and virtuous young woman, so naive is he. If this is symbolic of his general blindness to the facts of the case, it also suggests the perfunctory scrutiny of her features we might expect from someone who is more powerfully attracted to his own sex. Colley's description of Rogers is made more tellingly erotic than anything he says about Zenobia. But we can take the difference between Zenobia's would-be alluring facade and the comically squalid reality e.g. of her encounter with Talbot in his cabin, as expressive of the novel's wider concern with the dangerous and irrational things going on underneath an apparently rational or presentable surface. If Rogers's real beauty has its dangers, so does Zenobia's fake charm.

Mr Prettiman

Given the novel's preoccupation with the power of irrational desires, and the complex relationship between appearances and realities, Mr Prettiman does more than add a delicious strand of comedy to the novel. He offers a kind of commentary on the action, particularly on the causes of Colley's downfall.

Prettiman is a free-thinker i.e. a rationalist who doubts or even denies the existence of God, and who challenges the established social order. That is why Talbot has been deputed to watch over his movements, in case he should attempt to spread these doctrines in the colonies. The government of the period was perhaps the most reactionary England has ever known, partly in response to the alarming consequences of the revolution in France, where the king and a large section of the aristocracy and bourgeoisie had been executed, and an unstable republic set up – a republic eventually dominated, then overthrown, by Napoleon. There were many forces behind the revolution, but not the least were the rationalist philosophers of 18th-century Europe, whose main doctrine was that humanity could be indefinitely improved, if only the old repressive order were abolished. Prettiman is an English descendant of such thinkers, at least in the eyes of conventional men such as Talbot, and therefore potentially dangerous.

In fact, Prettiman's threat is largely mitigated by his absurd naivety. His refusal to accept the significance of superstitions, such as throwing salt over the shoulder (Chapter X) which seems reasonable at the time, is eventually shown to be, as Talbot puts it, an irrational rationalism, in that it too dismissively excludes the possibility of a realm of experience outside logic and common sense. This becomes most painfully and comically apparent when Prettiman misunderstands the report of Billy Rogers' conversation (page 273), taking the act of fellatio for the venial sin of chewing tobacco. The point here is not just that Prettiman misunderstands the vocabulary and the meaning: it is, after all, a reasonable mistake for someone to make under the circumstances. The comedy results in part from the fierce certainty with which he makes his point and our realization that, even were he to know the truth of the matter, the undeniably virtuous Prettiman could never begin to understand the powers which drive a man to act as Colley did. If he cannot comprehend the necessity of minor vices – alcohol and tobacco – how could he ever take in such an act of monstrous degradation, as it would certainly seem to him? As for the notion, dimly gleaned by Talbot, that such behaviour, however sordid, might direct us to a vital truth about the nature of Man, that would be quite beyond Prettiman. This is partly what Talbot means when he says that he will keep more of an eye on the future Mrs Prettiman than he will on her husband: he recognizes that, for all her primness (and her own failure to absorb the meaning of Colley's disgrace) Miss Granham is a stronger character who sees a little deeper than her free-thinking fiancé.

Prettiman's strength, then, is that he refuses to condone such behaviour as the carnival surrounding Colley's immersion. His weakness is the refusal to recognize the enormous power of the emotions which generate such occasions. These are the strengths and limitations of extreme rationalism, and they are one part of the wide spectrum of attitudes which the book presents, from logic to superstition, from cerebration to animal life, from worldly sophistication to tragic naivety.

Mr Brocklebank

As Zenobia is the antithesis to Miss Granham, so Brocklebank is the comic foil of Mr Prettiman: a parody of the 'artist' as Prettiman is a parody of the 'rationalist'. Brocklebank fits the stereotype of the lazy, drunken, loose-living artist, and Golding clearly enjoys – as he often does – a few digs at his own role as 'creator'.

Brocklebank's charm is that he is a fraud who admits to his fraudulence, or at least is not ashamed of it. In private life he makes only token efforts to conceal his relationships with two women companions and his fondness for drink; and in the long discussion about his work in chapter Gamma, it is made plain that economic and other considerations are at least as important as artistic values. For Brocklebank, painting is a living, and a rather precarious one at that; and it is a living which depends upon the ability to produce convincing illusions, rather as Zenobia's does. As she flatters her men, so Brocklebank must pander to his clients: would-be naval heroes who want to see themselves in the forefront of his pictures, however little such a posture may conform to reality. On the other hand, it appears that even to produce an imitation of reality in painting, it is necessary to introduce considerable distortion. These points underline the book's emphasis on the problematic nature of reality and its relationship to representations of it, whether in words or pictures. For the diary we are reading claims to be just such a representation, yet Talbot comes to have serious doubts about its adequacy.

Such doubts are in sharp contrast to Prettiman's certainty that the world is as it appears to be; and while Brocklebank is a less morally worthy character than Prettiman, he is – in spite of himself – a more sharp-sighted one. We cannot claim this as a virtue for Brocklebank, of course: he remains an old reprobate. But it gives him an altogether more sympathetic role.

The crew

We are aware of the ship's company as a group, both through Talbot's eyes and, more especially, through Colley's; but a number of them emerge as individuals, including Summers, Cumbershum, Deverel, Rogers and Wheeler.

Summers

Summers is the most interesting officer aboard, apart from Captain Anderson. Having risen from the ranks he is, like so many of the novel's other characters, marginal, an outsider – and this gives him a distinctive view of his fellow officers. It also provides him with a sensitivity to the attitudes of the ordinary sailors which becomes important when he tries to warn Colley against venturing among them, and when he tries to persuade the Captain, on the board of enquiry, not to take his investigations too far. Summers is the only one of the officers who seems to have any moral sense, and this too marks him out as a superior figure.

We first see him in an encounter with Talbot which is to prove educational for both of them, when Talbot inadvertently but typically patronizes Summers by congratulating him on his imitation of gentlemanly manners. Ironically, most of the characters in the book see social roles as fixed by birth – ironically, because almost everyone involved is in the process of improving their lot by emigration – even Talbot himself. Summers is the only character who has already done this, and he therefore has a particular role to play. If we compare his response to Talbot with Miss Granham's on a similar occasion – she implicitly rebukes him immediately – we can see what this is; for Summers is in the delicate position of needing to conciliate the powerful – Anderson, Talbot – while feeling it his duty to speak the truth. He combines the two excellently, and behaves with more sensitivity than anyone else in the book, attempting to restrain Colley, guiding Talbot, humouring Anderson without grovelling to him. As if to pile irony on irony, this shows that there really are natural differences between men, but they are moral, not social. Summers is morally superior to all his social superiors.

Deverel

If the discerning Summers is on the way up socially and professionally, Deverel is on the way down. The man Talbot at first takes for his natural equal is indeed from a comparable background, but his once great family is now in decline, and as though to symbolize the fact, Deverel, for all his breeding, is a kind of thug, one of the main conspirators in the plot to humiliate Colley in the badger bag, and a vindictive enemy of Captain Anderson whom he resents for rebuking him on that occasion when, as Deverel sees it, Anderson himself opened the way to Colley's humiliation. Deverel's desire for revenge against Anderson is an important marker of the honour code by which such men as he and Talbot live. Unable to challenge a superior officer, he intends to resign the service in Australia and then call the Captain out to fight a duel. This appears to him of infinitely greater importance than what happens to Colley – as his callous remark about the parson's death (page 270) reveals. Deverel is the exact opposite of Summers, who has learnt that one must deserve rewards. Deverel lives on the credit of his family past, and abuses that credit by not living up to its promise. Talbot is clear-sighted enough to realize this, though he only does so because of his instinctive dislike of the bullying Deverel. Nevertheless, his rejection of Deverel shows the moral progress Talbot has made during the book.

Cumbershum

This minor figure serves, like Oldmeadow, to represent the average among the officers on an inferior ship. Aggressive, dim, decent enough in the ordinary way, he is neither a nice man nor a good one. His main role is to provide a butt for Talbot's ironic commentary early in the novel (see especially pages 20–25).

Wheeler

Wheeler, like Cumbershum, is less a character than a role, and a rather sinister one. On the one hand providing the passengers with their needs he is also the captain's spy aboard ship on the other – a dual role which suggests a kind of omnipresence. It is Wheeler who finds and replaces Zenobia's letter in Talbot's cabin, Wheeler who is in contact with the mysterious purser, Wheeler who tells the captain about Rogers. Finally, he disappears, almost certainly pushed overboard in revenge for his betrayal of Rogers. This strange life and violent death add another strand to the complex society of the ship, suggesting all that goes on out of sight. What most of the passengers see is only the surface: the mechanism of working relationships aboard is as invisible as the stinking ballast. At least one critic has suggested a comparison between Wheeler and Mephistopheles, prompted by the reference to Goethe's play *Faust* near the end of the novel (Mephistopheles provides Faust with whatever he wants but ultimately leads him to destruction). But Wheeler is not so much evil as morally neutral.

Billy Rogers

Moral neutrality is a phrase we might use to describe Rogers, the only ordinary seaman individualized in the book. Rogers is a superb animal: massive, handsome, virile. He seduces both Zenobia and Colley, almost without meaning to; and it is made clear from his cross-examination by the Captain that he is well-known for his sexual exploits with both sexes. This lack of strong sexual preferences is suggestive of a larger indifference, an amorality which is animal – and Rogers is described in terms which suggest a magnificent animal by both Talbot and Colley. Yet if, as the book implies, Rogers is responsible for Wheeler's death, he cannot be said to be morally neutral. On the contrary, as Colley discovered to his cost, such unreflective erotic power is positively destructive.

Themes

This novel can be said to revolve round the great issues of politics, religion and sex, and to show them as inextricably involved with one another. In superficial terms, the political theme is expressed in the conflict between Prettiman's radicalism and Talbot's Toryism. Prettiman is a subversive while Talbot works for the government. But this is a minor issue. The real political core of the novel depends upon two things: class distinctions and power relations. Class is apparent as a theme from the very first page of the novel, when Talbot's social origins are revealed; and we soon become aware that the intricate and tenacious network of class distinctions which governs English society has been transferred to the ship. A white line is drawn between superior and inferior passengers, which the latter may not cross. Talbot is acutely aware of which officers are his social equals and which not; and he offends both Summers and Miss Granham by patronizing them. His own power also depends upon his social origins, as he well knows when he goes to beard the captain who, though an authority aboard ship, must still bow to Talbot's credentials. These depend on the still higher social rank of Talbot's patron, Lord X, and his future employer, the Governor. They represent the top of a social tree which stretches up to the highest aristocracy and the monarch, and Talbot is, as it were, their representative aboard ship. At the bottom of this ladder are the poorest emigrants, such as East and Roundabout.

However, the situation is complicated by the existence of a parallel class structure among the ship's company, depending not on birth but on naval rank. The captain's authority is absolute; his officers participate in it; and at the bottom of this ladder are the ordinary sailors. We can add to these two structures a third, embodied in Colley, who represents the authority of the Church – an authority even Captain Anderson acknowledges when he realizes that things have gone too far. If Talbot's power is based on social class and Anderson's on his role in the navy, Colley's derives from the more equivocal source of divine dispensation, which Talbot and Anderson only half believe in. But if Colley shows that he can exert his influence, albeit indirectly, over the other two, the example of Rogers shows why. Rogers and Colley are both socially inferior to Talbot, and have no standing whatever in the eyes of the captain, but they both 'know' something which gives them a hold over the others, whom Rogers can threaten with scandal and Colley with divine displeasure. This demonstrates the instability of power relations, which depend, after all, on a consent whose gift has long been forgotten: the agreement of others to recognize it.

Another force which can overturn the normal social and class structures is sex. Zenobia is little better than a common prostitute, Rogers a semi-illiterate ordinary seaman; but both have the power to attract and subvert their superiors to a catastrophic extent. The strength of sexual desire, and its complex relation to power is amply demonstrated in Colley's downfall, and symbolized by the longing to go down on his knees before Rogers. Beauty is here seen to be stronger than the strongest moral, spiritual and social restraints. Religion, far from standing in the way, only encourages Colley by inflaming his emotions and disguising from him their true object. Similarly, the ludicrous misunderstanding between Colley and his would-be friend, when the parson thinks Talbot is praying strenuously, suggests that Talbot, too, might use religion more consciously as a cover for his activities. Talbot, however, is due for a fall. Having regarded the church merely as a useful prop for the authority of the state, he has to learn that the mysteries religion tries to express, however mistakenly or crudely, really do exist, though their nature is veiled from us. There is more than simply what we see, as Talbot acknowledges on the novel's last page.

What, then, is the novel about? These are some of the themes, but it is more than a little difficult to disentangle them in a novel such as *Rites of Passage* without tearing its delicate texture; for although it is perfectly reasonable to say of this novel, as of any other, that it is 'about' something, it is a different matter when we come to say what that is. To begin with, the novel is narrated largely at second-hand, and partly at third-hand. The 'author' nowhere appears. Instead we have Talbot's story, and his narrative includes Colley's. In another sense, of course, the author is everywhere present, for it is he who chooses every word of the text; but where there is no obvious authorial guiding voice (as there is, for example, in novels by Jane Austen, Dickens, Tolstoy or Zola) then each reader has to do a good deal of interpretation for himself. We have to work out from the relationship between the two narratives – Talbot's and Colley's – what is important in the novel and what it is about.

This difficulty is further compounded by the fact that the centre of attention shifts as the text progresses. To begin with, we are naturally interested in Talbot, who offers us not only a sequence of events, but a commentary on that sequence, interpreting those events in his own way. But as time passes, we realize that Colley is really the centre of interest – and so profound is this shift that, for a considerable part of the book (60 pages out of 280) the story is told by Colley himself. Yet, by the end of the novel, the significance of this shift in emphasis is not at all clear, for the story's centre of gravity appears to have moved back to Talbot. What matters now is not so much Colley's tragedy, as Talbot's response to it, and the effects it has on him.

Bearing these complications in mind, then, we might say that the novel is about a number of themes, not all of them necessarily compatible, nor equally important to all readers. Clearly, the central action concerns Colley's mistreatment at the hands of the ship's company, lead by the captain, and the disastrous consequences this has on his hitherto repressed character. But once again, we are immediately faced with a difficulty. Are we to regard this as a tragedy or a black comedy? Is Colley really the centre of the action? And, if so, is he significant enough to be a tragic hero? The answer to the second question is almost certainly No. Horrible though Colley's predicament is, it is also described in comic terms almost throughout. The comedy is often savage, but at other times farce takes over. Colley even recognizes this himself. Yet the stubborn facts of his downfall and death at the hands of others remain – and the vital point that this downfall elicits from Colley a nobility at odds with the triviality of his behaviour at other moments, and his ludicrous appearance in the eyes of others. What are we to make of this apparent contradiction?

The answer lies in the narrative shift from Talbot to Colley, from outside to inside. What the book shows us is the simple but profoundly important point that tragedy and comedy depend largely on context and point of view. A figure of fun looks very different when we see the world with his eyes. Looked at from the outside, Colley is absurd, even contemptible. But, seeing that himself, Colley is shown to have a larger vision than his persecutors, for he is able to take in his own absurdity with other things: his sense of physical beauty, his intelligent observation of the other passengers, his acceptance of fate, and so on. And, in fact, he does not see himself as tragic, though he has a somewhat theatrical sense of missionary heroism which contributes to the catastrophe. But we, the readers, may perceive the tragic implications, for it is the audience's role to do that: we are able to take in both points of view, external *and* internal, and decide that, while

Colley's downfall has tragic elements, it is not a tragedy, but something more complicated. In other words, the important thing about the Colley episode is the combination of perspectives in which the reader can observe it.

Knowing this, we can say that the book is not primarily 'about' Colley, or even about Talbot: it is about the ways in which they perceive themselves and their relationship to others. And this 'theme' is evident in the treatment of all the characters. Take Captain Anderson, a misanthrope who keeps to his own quarters and resents approaches from the passengers. Both Talbot and Colley see Anderson as a kind of God, but this fills them with dismay, not respect or awe. Meanwhile, Anderson himself plays at being God, cultivating his plants and insisting on absolute authority over everyone aboard, however arbitrary. Yet, comparatively late in the book, we learn that this God is powerless: with the ending of the war he will probably be retired, he will lose his power and become an ordinary mortal. We suddenly see Anderson's fate as he sees it: lonely and futile. All the characters suffer this change of perspective in the reader's eyes as the narrative shifts round to reveal them in different lights, or as they see themselves. The aristocratic Deverel is discovered to be a lout, the sinister purser a harmless creditor, the obedient Wheeler a dangerous spy, the womanizing Rogers a homosexual, and so on. The degree to which this process is conducted through the character's own perception depends on his importance in the novel. Thus Colley and Talbot undergo the closest self-scrutiny, followed by Anderson. Minor figures, such as Zenobia, are revealed from the outside.

In a long complex story like *Rites of Passage* there are, of course, other themes, but they can all be viewed in terms of this dominant motif of shifting perspectives, for no absolute values are offered in the book, moral or spiritual. Consider again the question of religion, clearly a prominent theme here and throughout Golding's work. Colley believes passionately, as he thinks, in the established religion of his country: Anglican Christianity. But the conventionality of this belief, and the way in which it suddenly and alarmingly breaks down under pressure when Colley guesses what is going to happen to him, after his vision of the sun and moon balanced in the heavenly scales, hint that this belief is grounded partly in a *desire* to believe and the *convenience* of believing. And although we may interpret the final catastrophe in terms of the Christian myth of sacrifice – that one man should die for the people – it does not seem that Colley himself is sustained by this myth, in that he dies of shame, without ever confronting the problem. Moreover, it is one thing to be without sin, as Jesus was, and to die on behalf of others; it is quite another to perish as the result of a minor sexual offence, which, we are led to understand, goes on every day in the navy. The result is out of all proportion to the cause.

From such evidence, it might seem that Golding is telling the story of a man sadly deluded about the truth of ultimate reality. But the facts of the case are more complicated. Balanced against Colley's passionate faith is Talbot's tolerant, sceptical Erastianism; his acceptance of religion as a necessary aid to the authority of the state. He goes in the opposite direction to Colley – not to a belief in Christianity, certainly, but to an acknowledgement that there are more things in heaven and earth than reason can easily accommodate. And it is, ironically, the very episode which destroys Colley that draws Talbot to this conclusion. If men can be driven by such demons, then demons, in whatever form, must exist.

Yet Golding does not underwrite this conclusion either; and once again we are brought back to the question of narrative viewpoint. Colley's conclusion and Talbot's are just that: their conclusions, not an omnipotent author's. And that these conclusions are contingent, that they have no final force is strikingly confirmed by the fact that Golding has just published another novel dealing with the same character (Talbot) on the same ship, at a later stage. The first novel's ending, in other words, was provisional. We should be wary of drawing any lessons from it. If this can be said about all novels, other than the deliberately didactic, that only confirms the importance of remembering it when we are dealing with Golding.

The themes of novels, like the lessons we may learn from them, are, in part, a matter of reader's choice. It is, of course, up to the author whether he makes his intentions more or less explicit in this regard. There is no reason why a novelist should not announce his themes, if he has any, at the outset, and some novelists do just this. With Golding, we have the puzzle of an intensely serious writer, who often gives the impression of being didactic – and how could a professional schoolmaster not do this? – without specifying the content of his lesson. What seems to matter more is the strength of attention we give to the story. Even in *Free Fall* (1959) where Sammy, the narrator, announces from the beginning that he wants to answer a specific question. (When did I lose my freedom of action?) we are left at the end with more questions than answers – questions about the very nature of freedom, and about what it means to ask such questions. In

Rites of Passage the writer's proclaimed intention – to amuse his patron with an account of shipboard life – is at once fulfilled and contradicted. Nothing could be more gripping than the story with which Talbot is unexpectedly confronted, but it hardly conforms to the canons of 'amusement' he implies at the beginning of his narrative, when we are led to expect a light-hearted account of the freaks and foibles on the journey. Indeed, for much of the time this is what we actually get, and it forms a strangely powerful context for Colley's pathetic tale.

There is a sense in which this contradiction – between expectation and result – subtly leads us into another of the novel's themes: moral education. This is so much a part of traditional novels that one might almost say that the very idea of the novel is founded on it, in that the developing consciousness or the moral growth (they amount to much the same thing) of the main character or characters is something which occurs in almost any novel one can think of – even when represented by its absence i.e. the character's failure to grow. In *Rites of Passage* we have an interesting variation on this theme. Talbot develops considerably in awareness of others and his relationship to them, but at the end of the book, he is still perplexed by the meaning of these lessons. His moral sense, like his style, is enriched and darkened, but to what end? We are left with the question.

Style

Pastiche

Golding never writes an ordinary novel. Everything he does is experimental, especially in matters of style. *Rites of Passage* is no exception. To begin with, it is an historical novel in a vein Golding has not attempted before. He has set stories in the remote past (*The Scorpion God* and *Envoy Extraordinary*); in the recent past (*The Pyramid*); and even in prehistory (*Clonk Clonk*, and *The Inheritors*); but never in the middle distance. Nor has he attempted an extended pastiche – the detailed imitation of another literary style. In *Rites of Passage*, he does both.

The novel is set in the second decade of the nineteenth century, and its several styles reflect that setting, even down to the literary conventions used, and the complex allusions to other novels. The story takes the form of a journal, a common device in the eighteenth century, when the letter or diary mode was felt to give an immediacy to the narrative lacking in more formal approaches. Talbot's journal is, indeed, relatively informal, though only up to a point; we are also aware that he is cultivating an image for the benefit of his reader – Talbot's aristocratic patron – and for his own pleasure. He likes to think of himself as a worldly, tolerant, educated (but not academic) gentleman: amused, wise, superior, and sophisticated enough to deplore his own short-comings while rising above them. His particular trick is what one might call qualified cynicism: doubting the sincerity of motives – his own and other people's – but then charmingly withdrawing that doubt as unworthy, while letting it linger. Even his mother comes in for a touch of this on page 3, at the very opening of the story, when he is describing his departure from home. The point here is that Talbot well knows that his description echoes what a million other young men say on taking leave – and he wants us i.e. his readers, to know that he knows. And even if the journal is eventually to be for his eyes only – well, then, he wants to remind himself that he knows that he knows! After all, writing something or speaking it, is quite different from merely knowing or feeling it. By turning things into words we – paradoxically – give them a reality they did not possess; because language – unlike our feelings – is a public domain, and whatever enters it becomes public, even when uttered in private.

This rather complicated point is more important than it might at first seem, as the novel makes clear by constantly returning to the topic of records. Why, after all, bother writing down what we already know? Talbot keeps his journal, Colley writes a letter, Anderson makes notes in his log. And not only that: everything turns on what is recorded, what each of these men says about what has happened. Indeed, there is a sense that something only *has* happened when it is recorded, when people have access to a memory of it. If Talbot fails to tell Colley's true story – if he fails to preserve his journal and Colley's letter – that story will never be known. And in due course this has an effect on his style. Instead of going out of his way to make everything more amusing, he tries to concentrate on what he believes to be the truth. Instead of keeping a journal to convince his patron and himself what a very good chap he is, he turns instead to getting at the true meaning of his observations. Accordingly, his style becomes darker, richer; cheap cynicism is replaced by a profounder sense of irony.

The initial style of Talbot's journal is familiar, not so much from original journals of the period, but from sources which are already themselves imitations i.e. eighteenth- and nineteenth-century novels. In Emily Bronte's *Wuthering Heights*, for example; (an historical novel set in the same period) the principal narrator, Mr Lockwood, fancies himself just such a man as Talbot does. And it is clear that Talbot – like Lockwood – is modelling himself on such an image. The action of the novel reveals to him the inadequacy of this model, though not completely. Like *Wuthering Heights*, *Rites of Passage* ends with the narrator musing on a mystery, without either solving it or making clear what has happened to him as a result of the drama he has unearthed. However, Talbot's style in the part of the book after Colley's letter is subtly different, as we have noticed. In particular it suggests that Talbot is learning how to feel and how to record his feelings without coy embarrassment.

Feeling is present in Colley's letter from the beginning, in the form of another eighteenth-century literary convention: sensibility. This is just as artificial as Talbot's cultivation of cynicism, but it is an artifice which makes a virtue of sincerity and authenticity. Briefly: the doctrine of sensibility makes the capacity for feeling the most important human attribute. It claims, for example, that we will behave well if we follow the prompting of the heart; for men are naturally good and are only corrupted by the evils of the world they find themselves in. This is the opposite of Talbot's outlook; and Colley is by no means a whole-hearted advocate of sensibility. But his literary style, and the stance it indicates, are affected by the literary movement to which the cult of sensibility gave rise in the eighteenth century. Notice, for example, his awed descriptions of seascape, the near hysteria with which he records the moment when he kissed Talbot's cheek, and his reminiscences of home. Colley is an average eighteenth-century clergyman, tinged by sensibility, and ruined by homosexual urges he appears not to understand. The style of his writing appropriately alternates between sober good sense, deep feeling, pious resolution, and excessive emotion. In this context, his Christianity only works to undermine him by encouraging a vein of masochistic self-sacrifice. The image of going on his knees, often repeated and finally carried out with disastrous consequences, expresses this exactly.

Both Talbot's journal and Colley's letter are based on generalized literary models, then. The imitation is not close, but nevertheless brilliantly done. Golding does not worry himself over a few anachronisms, but concentrates on the spirit of the exercise with the purpose of rendering his story not so much veracious as dramatic. The style is used to underline the stages of the narrative. The same is true of smaller episodes in the story. Characters are carefully differentiated by their styles of speech, and here Golding again follows literary precedent. The dry formality of Miss Granham, the pedantry of Prettiman, the rambling verbosity of Brocklebank, the absurd theatricality of Zenobia, all have models, not only in the novels of the period, but in many before and since. One can find plenty of Zenobias in Dickens, for example, and Prettimans, too. In fact there is a good case for suggesting that Golding learnt to parody not from the 18th-century novels on which the styles of Talbot and Colley are based, but from nineteenth-century writers, more especially Dickens and Thackeray.

Literary allusion

The question of literary sources is of more than passing interest for the reader of *Rites of Passage*, given the extraordinary number of explicit and implicit allusions. On the very first page of the book Talbot not only manages to mention four English novelists: he does so in a context which is to prove important for our understanding of the text. Talbot distinguishes between 'lively' and sentimental writers – the second type belonging with the cult of sensibility described above. And while admitting the importance of feeling he also implies that it needs to be balanced by 'liveliness' i.e. rational understanding (in fact, Fielding, too, can be classified as sentimental, but that is by the way). The question of what this balance is and how to achieve it, are central preoccupations in the novel. Colley's death teaches Talbot – with the help of Summers – how to feel rightly; but it turns out that such feeling is also a matter of right thinking. Sentiment and liveliness need to be balanced in a way native to neither Colley nor Talbot, when the book begins.

That, at least, would be the conclusion were this novel – unthinkable prospect – by Jane Austen or Walter Scott, the major English novelists of the period, who both subscribe to a classical ideal of harmonious human nature. But the novel contains another set of allusions which suggest a rather different conclusion – allusions to the romantic poets also writing at this time. A text often quoted or cited is Coleridge's *Ancient Mariner*, an obvious choice in the context, but a confusing one, in that its own meaning is not at all clear. In it, the mariner shoots an albatross and his fellow sailors perish as a result. The mariner lives on, oppressed by the sense of sin, until he finds himself looking on brilliantly coloured water snakes and blessing them 'unawares'. Eventually he returns to land where he is compelled to wander the world telling his story to every stranger he meets.

Talbot alludes directly to the poem, but Colley's narrative is filled with veiled references to it – most strikingly when he describes the simultaneous rising of the sun and moon, vital symbols in Coleridge's tale. However we interpret the poem, it seems to be about sin and salvation, a common theme in Golding's work. The mariner's compulsive story-telling is also echoed in Talbot's determinaton to keep his journal, as a witness to the truth of events which are as strange and monstrous as the events of the poem. The notion of sacrifice is also present in both works, in that a solitary figure is seen somehow to be paying the price for the sins of his fellows. The poem, like the novel, is concerned with issues of free-will and determinism: both the mariner and Colley are driven to acts – shooting the albatross, fellatio – with dire consequences; and both experience Grace, that involuntary awareness of God's infinite power and mercy, expressed in very similar language (compare Coleridge's water snakes with Colley's vision of the sea on page 247). But it would be unwise to press parallels too far; for one thing, Coleridge's poem has a positive Christian content lacking in *Rites of Passage*. It is better to concentrate on the suggestive similarities of detail between poem and novel, rather than to press any overall comparison too hard. Perhaps the important point is the contrast between this romantic work and the eighteenth-century novels alluded to – a contrast which supports and refines the larger structural distinctions between reason and feeling, detachment and commitment, so important in the book.

After all, *The Ancient Mariner* is only one of many writings referred to in the text. Equally important are the references to Greek literature, especially tragedy. Homer is quoted by both Talbot and Colley, but significantly the first uses the original Greek (partly to show off, partly to patronize a midshipman, partly because it comes naturally), while Colley cites an English translation of the *Odyssey*. Appropriately, the poem is about a sea-journey, in which Odysseus and his men search for the fabulous treasure of the Golden Fleece, but the reference is not explored.

The allusions to Greek tragedy, however, are of vital importance. Although Colley mentions Sophocles, it is Talbot who meditates on the idea that what he is witnessing is a kind of play, and the novel is filled with theatrical language. He talks of what is happening to Colley in terms of acts and scenes, refers to Zenobia as putting on a performance, considers himself as audience and critic, and so on. This habit suggests a number of possibilities, of which the most obvious is Talbot's evolution from spectator to participant in the 'drama'. Beginning as a detached observer he is gradually drawn into the action, without ever completely losing the trick of viewing himself from the outside. But this alteration in role transforms his perspective, compelling him – perhaps for the first time in life – to reflect on what it is to be a victim, not a bystander. But Greek tragedy also suggests an idea of Fate: the idea that the gods have preordained what is to happen, and that there is no escape from what is to happen. In this instance, we need not think of Fate as an external agency – the gods, or even God – but in terms of the little world of the ship, filled with conflicting desires and urges. Part of the force urging Colley on to his destiny is also within: the homosexual desire which brings about his shame. Most important of all, what happens to him happens because of the man he is and the circumstances he is in. It would not happen to another type of man, nor perhaps to Colley in another time and place.

The question Golding asks is whether men are fated by their circumstances or not. Are we all acting in a play, the script of which has been already and immutably written? Or do men have the freedom to choose, within their limited sphere? To choose a course of action other than the one apparently laid down? Ironically, the paths of Talbot and Colley cross on this issue. The privileged Talbot, who has seen himself as one of the fortunate who can choose to make of their lives what they will, discovers that one cannot avoid certain moral choices, whatever the material circumstances of life, if one is to go on thinking of oneself with any self-esteem. Colley on the other hand, who passionately submits himself to the will of God, is destroyed by the eruption of an unexpected desire which suggests a wilfulness altogether at odds with submission. Are we free, or are we not? The novel does not say, but the allusions to Greek tragedy persistently return us to the question.

The discussion is enriched by two further sets of allusion. The Bible is naturally a text to which Colley resorts, contrasting it favourably with the so-called wisdom of rationalist philosophers. Talbot makes a similar contrast, the other way round: his preferred authority is the eminently rational Aristotle. Ironically, the biblical view of divine providence as the unexpected intervention of God in human affairs is borne out by Colley's tragic fate. Determined to preach the Word to the pagans among the crew, he is destroyed by his recklessness.

Where Colley refers to the Bible, Talbot prefers Shakespeare (a point he makes himself at the bottom of page 262). Shakespeare is Talbot's favourite writer, and one he frequently compares with his patron's favourite Racine, whom his lordship has even translated. Once again, these allusions confirm our view of Talbot as a man inclined to look at life – and thereby to distance himself from it – through literature, which he even uses to conceal, or substitute for, his own responses. But the choice of Shakespeare over Racine is more specific. From the early eighteenth century onwards, these two playwrights have been cited as the most distinguished and characteristic products of their cultures. Racine is formal, intense, and unremitting in his view of life as, at best, a desperate business, more likely to end badly than well. Shakespeare, by contrast, appears to believe in the redeeming quality of love, even in his darkest tragedies. Now we might expect the cynical Talbot to prefer the aristocratic gloom of Racine. The fact that he does not suggests that he is more inclined to the 'sentimental' view of life than he usually cares to admit. And indeed, if we reread the first pages of the book carefully, we can see that much of Talbot's debonair detachment is an assumed pose. He really is, as he says himself, 'a good enough fellow at bottom'.

Imagery and symbolism

Talbot assiduously cultivates a style rich in imagery, and it is important to be aware of this. In particular, many of Talbot's phrases have a strong symbolic quality about them: they appear to mean much more than their literal sense. This is significant in a story which brings its own narrator to a realization that there is indeed more to things than meets the eye. A persistent stream of images is concerned with reading and translation: whether one language can ever be turned into another; whether one person can ever understand another, even speaking the same language; whether experience can be rendered adequately in words; and whether one can make sense of experience by translating it into logical structures. At the beginning of the novel Talbot, despite his occasional self-deprecating remarks, is confident about his ability to handle language: he coins witty phrases, quotes in Greek, makes dozens of literary allusions. By the end, he is still offering pyrotechnics, but the confidence has gone, and the novel's last words hint at the ultimately incomprehensible nature of things – a common theme in Golding.

One aspect of the preoccupation with language is the deployment of different specialist vocabularies: painting and literature are both discussed; and class diction also plays a part; but the most interesting example is what Talbot calls Tarpaulin – the sailors' language, specially developed for life aboard ship. Naturally, boats and sailing play an important part in the imagery. If, as Colley observes, the sailors seem to have a world of their own, expressed in their language, the ship is a world for the passengers too, and the comparison is frequently made: they are making the journey of life aboard this fragile vessel – historically this must be one of the commonest images, and not only in literature. The first sailing epic – Homer's *Odyssey* – is quoted; but more important is the physical being of the ship they are in: rotten, dark, stinking, quite likely to crack up in a major storm, and ridden with the petty passions and rivalries which rule the larger world. If the sailors communicate their own feelings and ideas in their mysterious language, even the other passengers find themselves falling into seafaring ways. They become a community or series of communities – a point made clear by the different gatherings described in the book.

But symbolism also operates on a more detailed level, and we are made aware of it by Talbot himself – Zenobia's paint, the captain's flowers, the smelly darkness in which the purser dwells, Mr Prettiman's hair, Miss Granham's hat, Billy Rogers's naked torso, Colley's vestments – all have a story to tell beyond their immediate significance. They, too, constitute a kind of language, a language of signs, which tell the careful observer far more than any kind of words. It is not what Zenobia says or does which reveals her nature to Talbot, but the way she looks and speaks. Brocklebank's drunken semi-nakedness communicates something quite different to Colley's. No-one is much surprised by it and therefore no-one is very shocked. But Colley's bare legs symbolize his fall from virtue, his complete abandonment of respectable society, as surely as the simultaneous presence in the sky of sun and moon symbolizes for him the scales of divine justice.

Structure

The central event is Colley's downfall, and this determines the novel's structure by means of the double narrative through which we learn about it.

The Colley episode itself falls into three parts: the clergyman's unfortunate first encounters with Captain Anderson; his humiliating immersion in the badger bag; and his expedition below decks. In each part, Colley is exposed to brutal, degrading treatment, and dies, it seems, as a direct result of his exploit with Billy Rogers. The tripartite structure is reflected in the larger structure of the novel, in which Talbot first observes Colley from the outside, then learns about him from his letter, and finally experiences a deepening of his understanding as a result. Colley dies, Talbot lives. The difference points up the symmetries and the asymmetries between the two three-part structures. Both begin by making mistakes – Talbot about his fellow passengers, Colley, more painfully, about the Captain. Each then has a devastating experience – immersion in the badger bag, and the reading of Colley's letter. Each then proceeds to defy the captain's bullying – Colley by extracting an apology, Talbot by refusing to condone the results of the enquiry and keeping his own journal. The final outcome is disaster and death for Colley. While Talbot lives, his life is not the same. Colley's words – what a man does defiles him – apply equally to Talbot: what a man does, or does not do, remains with him for life.

This reflection of Colley's progress in the larger structure of Talbot's development underlines the complex connections between the two men whose destinies, though very different, nevertheless echo one another; and it also reminds us to be careful about what we take to be central in the book. If Colley's downfall is the central event, or series of events, both literally and in terms of the attention devoted to it, the novel is equally 'about' Talbot and his reactions to that downfall. Colley and Talbot live, as it were, for one another: their lives only have meaning in relation to one another. There is a perpetual interplay between their moments of ignorance and illumination. Having confronted Anderson, for example, Colley appears to have triumphed, but his triumph is only the prelude to a steeper fall. Understanding the truth about Colley, Talbot appears to have the whip hand over Anderson, but this dominance is qualified by Talbot's newly-acquired sense of his own fallibility. Both men have to learn that their fates are in other hands than their own: Wheeler's, Anderson's, Summers's, even Billy Rogers's.

Colley's narrative forms a kind of climax, built up to by Talbot's account of what happens to him, and succeeded by the court of enquiry in which the truth begins to emerge, and a final, throw-away scene in which the nature of Colley's shame is suddenly revealed to Talbot. The build-up is comparatively gentle. Only as Talbot becomes disoriented about time do things begin to accelerate – and the manipulation of time is important in the novel, which stretches out some moments, and passes rapidly over others. Gradually we become aware that the novel is not about Talbot but about Colley. Then we revise our estimate: it is about both, and the unlikely relationship – or lack of it – between them. The temperature of the writing rises rapidly when Colley's story begins – but perhaps the most interesting thing about the book's structure is that the crucial event – Colley's act of fellatio with Rogers – is missing from both narratives. It is only much later, almost as an afterthought, that we discover it. The mystery this creates – we know neither the crime nor the culprit until near the end of the book – naturally intrigues us and helps to throw the weight of the story not onto what happened to Colley but on his response to it, and on Talbot's response to that response. This makes us concentrate on the uncertainties of the situation. The urbane Talbot, valued by patron and government precisely because he knows how to handle awkward situations (and priding himself on the ability) knows neither what has happened, nor why it has had such a result. It is only on the very last page of the book that he reaches an explicit conclusion – that a man can die of shame – but this conclusion only throws us back into another mystery. Why should Colley have done such a thing? How can he know his own nature so little, when its homoerotic tendencies have been revealed to us so often in his letter. Above all – if there is a divine providence, how can it play such a dirty trick?

This question is a fundamental one for both Colley and Talbot who each, for their different reasons and in their different ways, have subscribed to the view that there is an order in the universe and that it must be maintained. But the very structure of the book questions this, by reaching no conclusion, by leaving the question of what has happened open. If there is a meaning in poor Colley's downfall, it is yet to seek – a conclusion brought home to us by the way in which the truth of the matter is constantly postponed. Only on the penultimate page does Talbot make it clear that an act of fellatio was the main cause of Colley's shame – but by that time we have been drawn into a series of doubts which we cannot shake off. Both narratives begin in confidence of a certain position, and while Colley's letter ends on a note of confidence, his life concludes in mortal shame. Talbot's life continues, but his narrative ends on a profoundly disturbing note – and ends at all only because he has come to the end of his note-book. The implication is that more paper for further reflection might take him deeper into the mire of uncertainty.

General questions

1 Give an account of the ways in which Talbot changes or develops during the novel.

Guideline notes

Talbot's personality at first as revealed by his style: witty, worldly, cultivating cynical detachment. Also patronizing, snobbish, complacent.
By the end he is still worldly, but sceptical rather than cynical, much more sympathetic, less rationally secure, aware of mystery in life.
This is brought about by his increasing involvement with Colley's disaster. At first he finds the parson absurd and obnoxious, but begins to feel sorry for him. Then tries to help in a casual way. Then under pressure from Summers, makes more effort. When it's too late he's shocked into a realization of what has happened.
This shock affects him emotionally and morally, makes him determined to have justice for Colley.
His journal becomes more than an amusement: it is also evidence, and a testimony.
Note the changes in tone and style – the later journal is darker, more emotional, less confident.

2 Describe the relationship between Colley and Talbot. What do they mean to one another?
3 What is the difference between Summers's notion of *noblesse oblige* and Talbot's idea of Justice?
4 How guilty of Colley's death is Captain Anderson?
5 What part do descriptions of the ship play in the novel?
6 Is the joke about the purser relevant or irrelevant to the main plot?
7 Compare the two women characters and their roles.
8 How important are class distinctions in the book?
9 What views of Christianity appear in the novel, and what part do they play?
10 How important are the sexual acts in this novel?
11 Describe the style of the novel's opening pages and account for it.

12 To what extent does the style of Colley's letter reveal his personality and in what ways?
13 What would you describe as the climactic moment or moments in the book – and why?
14 Are there any analogies or structural parallels between Talbot's enlightenment and Colley's downfall?
15 In your own words, describe the structure of the book. (Refer to the section on Structure in these notes.)

Further Reading

Golding – *Close Quarters* (Faber, 1987)

Golding – *Darkness Visible* (Faber, 1979)

Golding – *Lord Of The Flies* (Faber, 1954)

Golding – *The Spire* (Faber, 1964)

Golding – *Lord of the Flies* ed. G. Handley (Brodie's Notes)

Baker, J. in *Twentieth Century Literature* vol. 28 no. 2 (interview with Golding)

Crompton, D. *A View from the Spire* (includes an essay on *Rites of Passage*) (Blackwell, 1984)

Pemberton, C. *William Golding* (a useful brief introduction to the earlier work) (Longmans, 1969)